LIST
OF THE
TREES, SHRUBS AND LARGE CLIMBERS

LIST
OF THE
TREES, SHRUBS AND LARGE CLIMBERS
FOUND IN THE
DARJEELING DISTRICT, BENGAL

J. S. GAMBLE, M. A.

GYAN

Published by

GYAN

Gyan Publishing House
5, Ansari Road
Daryaganj, New Delhi-110002
Phone: 011-47034999, 9811692060
E-mail: books@gyanbooks.com

Distribution Network
gyanbooks.com
India, USA, Canada, UK, Australia, France

ISBN: 978-81-212-8488-2 (PB)
First Published, 1878

2nd Impression 2023

Printed at: Gyan Press, Delhi.

LIST OF THE TREES, SHRUBS AND LARGE CLIMBERS
Author: J. S. GAMBLE

LIST

OF THE

TREES, SHRUBS, AND LARGE CLIMBERS

FOUND IN THE

DARJEELING DISTRICT, BENGAL.

By J. S. GAMBLE, M.A.,

ASSISTANT CONSERVATOR OF FORESTS, BENGAL

Calcutta:

PRINTED AT THE BENGAL SECRETARIAT PRESS

1878.

PREFACE.

In January 1873, when on tour in the Darjeeling Terai with Dr. W. Schlich, the Conservator of Forests in Bengal, we found considerable difficulty in determining the names of the large number of different species of trees which we came across. The native names did not help us much. No Paharia,* Lepcha, or Mechi names were to be found in such books as were then available, and of which Balfour's "Timber Trees" was the principal. We then determined to commence at once to collect specimens, as well as notes on the native names and on the economic uses of which we could obtain any information. The information thus collected is by no means complete, and it would scarcely have been published so soon had it not been for my transfer from Darjeeling, and the consequent orders of the Government of Bengal that I should prepare as complete a list as possible before leaving. Only about six weeks have, however, been available for the work, and the result is that the list is very incomplete; but I hope that Darjeeling Forest Officers will not allow the collection of data to drop, but add to the information herein given such further notes as they may be able to make with a view to the ultimate preparation of a more complete list. There are many gentlemen about Darjeeling, especially planters, from whom I have received much information; and I have no doubt that many of them would again consent to help and add any facts which may come before them. For the determination of the scientific names I am indebted to the kindness of Dr. G. King, the Superintendent,

* The emigrants from the eastern parts of Nepal who have settled in the Darjeeling district are called "Paharias."

and Mr. Sulpiz Kurz, the Curator, of the Herbarium at the Royal Botanical Gardens, Calcutta; and Mr. C. B. Clarke, M.A., of the Educational Department, has given me much help by a nearly complete set of his own Darjeeling collection. Specimens of almost all the plants mentioned in this list have been filed by me in the office of the Conservator of Forests, Bengal, and will be always available for inspection and consultation.

In cases where there is any doubt of the correct scientific name, either generic or specific, it has been written in brackets: thus—

(*Melia composita*, Willd.) means that both the correct generic and specific names are uncertain, but that I consider it may possibly be that species.

Acacia (*ferruginea*, DC.) means that though the plant undoubtedly belongs to the genus "Acacia," yet it is not quite certain, though very probable, that it is the species "ferruginea, DC."

The native names must be received with a certain amount of caution. "Lepcha" names are generally to be pretty well depended on; but those given by Paharias as often as not are given on the spur of the moment, and in many cases merely invented to mean "a pretty tree," "bitter leaves," "medicine bark," or some such name, derived only from the appearance or use of the plant. Paharias, too, especially "chaprasis" or other servants, on being questioned, often think they are bound to give a name of some kind, especially if they think the questioner is anxious to find one, and consequently invent them for the plant on the spur of the moment, quite as readily as they invent new names for themselves at each place where they find work. I have done my best to verify constantly the correctness of the names given, but I have very little doubt but that in many cases they will prove to be wrong, or at any rate useless, as already described. The following are the letters used to designate the different languages: *P.=Paharia, L.=Lepcha, H.=Hindi, Bg.=Bengali, Bh.=Bhutia.*

In the description of size of tree, I have used the formula invented by Mr. Kurz in his "Preliminary Forest Report of Pegu," only considerably simplified. The letters E. and L. denote "evergreen" and "leaf-shedding" respectively; and, as an example of how the formula is to be read—

L. $\frac{100\text{-}120}{60\text{-}80+10\text{-}15}$ means a leaf-shedding tree growing to the height of from 100 to 120 feet, having a clear stem of from 60 to 80 feet, and an average girth, at four feet from the ground, of from 10 to 15 feet.

The letters denoting forest are thus explained :—

S. F.=Sâl forest.

K. S. F.=Khair and Sissu forest.

Sv. F.=Savannah forest.

M. P. F.=Mixed plains forest. This may be either *w.*, "wet," like the "Dalka Jhar;" or *d.*, "dry," like the forests about the Balasun river, and between it and the Hurlia nadi.

L. H. F.=Lower hill forest, generally found from the plains to 3,000 feet elevation. It may be "ridge" forest, or "valley" forest.

M. H. F.=Middle hill forest, generally found between 3,000 and 6,000 feet.

U. H. F.=Upper hill forest, from 6,000 to 8,000 feet, sometimes called "oak" forest.

R. F.=Rhododendron forest, about 8,000 to 10,000 feet.

F. F.=Fir forest, generally from 9,000 to 12,000 feet.

These different kinds of forests were described by Dr. Schlich in his "Memorandum on the Forests of Sikkim" in 1873, and by myself in an article in the "Indian Forester," Vol. I, No. 2.

The flowering and fruiting seasons are described by the number of the months, thus: fl. 3, fr. 7, mean "flowers in March and ripens its fruit in July."

The present list merely relates to the political district of Darjeeling, a district which is separated on the north from Sikkim by the Rumaun, Great Rangít, and Rangpo rivers; on the west from Nepal by the Singalila mountain range and the Mechi River; and on the east from Bhutan by the Jaldoka River. To the south lie the British districts of Purneah and Julpigori.

In conclusion, I would suggest the application of a similar plan of local lists of trees to other divisions of the provinces of Bengal and Assam: they would prove of great value if ever a forest flora of North-Eastern India is compiled to complete the series of forest floras already published for Madras, Burma, and North-Western and Central India.

J. S. GAMBLE.

DARJEELING,
The 31*st March* 1877.

LIST

OF THE

TREES, SHRUBS, AND LARGE CLIMBERS

FOUND IN THE

DARJEELING DISTRICT, BENGAL.

RANUNCULACEÆ.

Clematis smilacifolia, Wall. Climber of the M. Hills up to 5,000 ft. Fl. 10; red, very handsome.

Clematis Gouriana, Roxb. Climber of Terai forests, and up to 3,000 ft. Fl. 9.

Clematis acuminata, DC. Climber; common about 4,000 and up to 7,000 ft. Fl. 9-12.

Clematis Buchananiana, DC. *Tungbongrik, L.* Climber of M. and U. H. F. 5,000 to 10,000 ft. Fl. 10-12; cream colour.

Clematis grewiæflora, DC. Climber of M. and U. H. F. 5,000 to 7,000 ft. Fl. 11-1; very woolly.

Clematis montana, Ham. Climber of U. H. F. about 7,000 to 8,000 ft. Fl. 7.

Naravelia Zeylanica, DC. Climber of Terai, near streams and L. H. F. up to 3,000 ft. Fl. 5-7, fr. 10.

DILLENIACEÆ.

Dillenia Indica, L. *Chalta, P.*; *Phamsikol, L.* E. $\frac{30\text{-}40}{10\text{-}20+4\text{-}5}$ of the M. P. F. *w.* in Terai and L. H. F. valleys. Fl. 9, fr. 3-4. Bark red, peeling off in large flakes, and easily recognized in the swamp forests, where the leaves are only seen with difficulty. Wood red-brown, hard, heavy, with numerous medullary rays; rarely used. Fruit very large, like a big apple; outside formed of the fleshy leaves of the calyx; is not unpleasant when nearly ripe. Flowers white, very big. Leaves big, rough, with numerous parallel veins.

DILLENIA PENTAGYNA, Roxb. *Tatri, P.*; *Akshi, M.*; *Shuknikúng, L.* L. $\frac{40\text{-}60}{10\text{-}30+5\text{-}8}$ of the S. F., Sv. F. and M. P. F. *d.* of Terai and L. H. F. ridges and plateaux up to 3,000 ft. Fl. 4, fr. 5-6. Bark white-brown, peeling off in round rather thick flakes, and leaving a white colour beneath. Stem often irregularly shaped on the section, and in hill forests much buttressed. Wood reddish brown, resembling but lighter coloured than that of the preceding, and both rather resembling "beech" in consistency and qualities; they are, however, very liable to warp unless thoroughly seasoned. It makes very good charcoal. Flowers yellow, small; appear before the leaves. Fruit yellow, ripe at the time the leaves appear; not unpleasant to eat when green. Leaves very large, parallel-veined, venate. This tree seems to indicate a bad soil when found with Sâl, and in the Sâl and Savannah forests it is usually small, while on the hills it grows to be a very large fine tree.

DELIMA SARMENTOSA, Linn. *Monkyourik, L.* E. climber of L. H. F. valleys; not common. Has very rough leaves.

MAGNOLIACEÆ.

MAGNOLIA CAMPBELLII, Hk. f. and Th. *Lal Champ, P.*; *Sigumgrip, L.*; *Pendder, Bh.* L. $\frac{60\text{-}80}{30\text{-}50+10\text{-}12}$ of the U. H. F. from 7,000 to 10,000 ft. Common on Senchal and Tongloo. Fl. 4, fr. 9-10. Bark very dark coloured, that of the branches almost black. Wood yellow, good for house-building, but scarce now and not so good as the wood of *Michelia excelsa*, which is much more common. Flowers large, 6-10 in. diameter; rose or white appear before the leaves. Fruit with red seeds, which if sown in November germinate in May. It is being grown at Rungbool nursery.

MAGNOLIA GLOBOSA, Hk. f. and Th. $\frac{E}{L}$ (?) big tree; not uncommon in the inner valleys of the Singalila range, such as those of the Rithoo and Siri, at about 9,000 to 10,000 ft. Often seen in the midst of dense bamboo thickets.

MICHELIA CATHCARTII, Hk. f. and Th. *Kala Champ, P.*; *Atokdung, L.* E. $\frac{60\text{-}80}{20\text{-}30+4\text{-}8}$ of the M. and U. H. F. from 5,000 to 7,000 ft., but rare above 6,000 ft., though very common below that elevation, and especially about Dumsong. Fl. 6, fr. 10-11. Seeds orange-yellow. Heartwood dark, black-green, soft, easily worked, good for house-building. Sapwood white, much attacked by insects. Flowers terminal, white; turn deep red in drying. Leaves small.

MICHELIA LANUGINOSA, Wall. *Gogay Champ, P.* L. $\frac{40\text{-}80}{20\text{-}30+4\text{-}8}$ of the M. and U. H. F. from 5,000 to 7,000 ft., with the preceding. Common in Darjeeling station. Fl. 9, fr. 12-1. Wood greyish white. Bark greyish brown, smooth. Flowers white. Seeds orange-red. Leaves soft pubescent, long.

Michelia excelsa, Bl. *Bara Champ, P.*; *Safed Champ, P.*; *Gok, Bh.*; *Sigugrip, L.* L. $\frac{60\text{-}100}{40\text{-}50+10\text{-}15}$ of the U. H. F. from 6,000 to 8,000 ft. Fl. 3, fr. 10. Wood yellow, turning yellow-brown with exposure; light, close-grained, easily worked; used for all purposes of building, but chiefly for planks, window frames, door frames and panels, also to make tables and chairs. It has a very strong smell when freshly cut. Flowers large, white, sweet-scented. Seeds red, very oily. Ripe in November, and if sown then germinate in May and June. It is being largely grown at Rungbool for plantation purposes, and the seedlings seem to require several shiftings, and to be kept at least three years in nursery before transplanting.

Michelia champaca, Linn. *Oulia Champ, P.* E. $\frac{60\text{-}100}{40\text{-}50+8\text{-}12}$ of the L. H. F. up to 3,000 feet. Sapwood white, soft; heartwood light yellow, with narrow medullary rays, rather large pores, and very distinct annual rings; stem very cylindrical, reaches 8 ft. girth at an age of 100 to 120 years. The timber is very good for planking, door and window frames, furniture, &c., and much in demand, but it is now rather rare, and big trees very scarce. A small quantity of seed has been sown at Bamunpokri.

Talauma Hodgsoni, Hk. f. and Th. *Patpatta, P.*; *Harré, P.*; *Siffoo-kúng, L.* E. $\frac{30\text{-}40}{15\text{-}20+3\text{-}6}$ of the L. and M. H. F. up to 6,000 ft., and of the M. P. F. *w.* in Terai (Dalka Jhar). Fl. 5, fr. 10. Wood white, but in very old trees it is quite black, especially the wood of the roots. It is used for "kukri" and "ban" handles, and for various other small wood purposes. Flowers terminal, large, the petals falling almost immediately after opening. Fruit large; seeds bright red; leaves very large.

Schizandra grandiflora, Hk. f. and T. *Singhatalara, P.*; *Taksielrik, L.* Large climber of U. H. F. from 6,000 to 10,000 ft. Fl. 5, fr. 6-7,—red, edible. Common round Darjeeling.

Schizandra elongata, Hk. f. and T. *Mandani—Singhata, P.*; *Flotoshingrik, L.* Climber of the U. H. F. Not so common as the preceding.

ANONACEÆ.

Uvaria macropoda, Hk. f. and T. *Rabu-lara, P.* Large woody climber of the L. H. F. about 2,000 to 3,000 ft. Fl. and fr. 9. Found at Mongpu.

Goniothalamus sesquipedalis, Hk. f. and T. *Sané, P.*; *Singnok-kúng, L.* E. small shrub, 3-6 ft. high, of M. P. F. *w.* (Dalka Jhar, &c.) in Terai and L. and M. H. F. up to 5,000 ft. Fl. and fr. at almost all seasons.

Anona squamosa, Linn. *Shariphal.* The custard-apple is found in cultivation in the Terai, and with a little care gives very good fruit.

Miliusa macrocarpa, Hk. f. and T. Small tree of the M. H. F. about 4,000 to 6,000 ft. Fl. 12-3, fr. 8-9. Not very common, but good specimens may be seen in the Tukdah Reserve.

Miliusa Roxburghiana, Hk. f. and T. *Sungden-kúng, L.* E. $\frac{15-25}{5-15+1-2}$ of the M. P. F. *w.* in Terai and L. H. F. valleys up to 2,000 ft. Fl. 4-5, fr. 7-8. Not uncommon. Bark grey to grey-brown, with small vertical dotted excrescences. Wood grey-white, with numerous lighter coloured medullary rays of all sizes; it is hard and heavy, and works well: cut parallel to the rays its markings resemble those of "bird's-eye" maple. The flowers are dark red, and the carpels round and long-stalked.

MENISPERMACEÆ.

Aspido carya uvifera, Hk. f. and T. *Pangla, P.*; *Myungarer-rik, L.* Climber of the M. H. F. about 5,000 ft. Fl. 5, fr. 7. Fruit eaten by Lepchas.

Parabœna sagittata, Miers. *Karpatilara, P.* Climber of the L. H. F. up to 3,000 ft. Fl. 5, fr. 9.

Tinospora cordifolia, Miers. *Gurjo, P.* Climber of the K. S. F. and waste places of the Terai. Fl. 2, when leafless. Bark grey-brown, warty. Wood very soft, consisting of alternate medullary rays and rows of big pores. It sends down long filiform roots from the branches of the trees over which it climbs. The wood is ground up and used by Paharias to cure cattle of pains in the stomach. Elephants are particularly fond of it, and in the Mahanadi khair-sissu forest last year (1875-76) I noticed several hundreds of good khair trees which had been pulled down by wild elephants to feed on the succulent stems of this creeper.

Stephania elegans, Hk. f. and T. Small wiry climber of the M. and U. H. F. about 5,000 ft. Fl. and fr. 11-12. The leaves are peltate, and have a curious metallic lustre beneath.

Stephania rotunda, Lour. *Nimi-lara, P.* A large bulbous-rooted climber of the L., M. and U. H. F. up to 6,000 ft. Fl. 4-5. Gives a fibre used by the Paharias for fishing-lines.

Cissampelos Pareira, Linn. *Batúlpati, P.* Large common climber of Terai and L. H. F. up to 3,000 ft. Fl. 8-9, fr. 10-11. It yields a strong fibre, used by Paharias.

BERBERIDEÆ.

Hollböllia latifolia, Wall. *Chiriyanangri, P.*; *Pronchadik, L.*; *Domhyem, Bh.* Large climber of the M. and U. H. F. and R. F. from 4,000 to 10,000 ft. Fl. 5, fr. 8-9. Outer bark corky, deeply cleft vertically to a quarter of an inch thick. Inner bark brown, hard. Wood loose-grained, but rather hard; very broad medullary rays and large pores. Fruit large, red, eagerly sought for by hill-men, who are very fond of it. There are two varieties, both of which are found in the station of Darjeeling.

Berberis Nepalensis, Spreng. *Chatri, P.* E. $\frac{15\text{-}20}{0\text{-}5+1\text{-}2}$ of the U. H. F., from 6,000 to 8,000 ft. Very common in the Rungbool forest and the station of Darjeeling, where it is often planted for ornament. Fl. 9-11, fr. 3-4. Bark soft, light brown, corky. Wood bright yellow, with fine medullary rays; hard, heavy. The wood is used, ground into a paste, by Paharias, to mark the caste-marks on their foreheads. It is easily recognized by its pinnate leaves with holly-like prickly leaflets, yellow flowers and blue glaucous berries.

Berberis umbellata, Wall. E. shrub of the Singalila range, about 10,000 to 11,000 ft. Fr. 9.

Berberis aristata, DC. *Tsema Bh.* E. small prickly-leaved shrub. Common on Tongloo, 10,000 ft., where it forms the chief undergrowth under the rhododendrons. Fl. 4-5, fr. 9-10.

Berberis concinna, Hk. f. *Tsema Bh. E.* small shrub, found with the preceding, but recognized from it by its red branches and leaves.

Berberis insignis, Hk. f. and T. *Timberjhien, L.* E. large shrub of the hill forests of Singalila and the higher points of the Dumsong Hills, about 8,000 to 10,000 ft. Fl. 4, fr. 10. Often cultivated for ornament, *e.g.* at Rungyrúm.

Berberis angulosa, Wall. *Chutra, P.* E. large shrub of Singalila range. Common on Suburkum, 11,000 ft. Fl. 4, fr. 10. Bark brown, rather corky. Wood yellow-brown, hard, close-grained, with very narrow annual rings.

CAPPARIDEÆ.

Capparis pumila, Champ. E. shrub of the L. H. F. valleys, up to 3,000 ft. Fl. 9.

Capparis multiflora, Hk. f. and T. *Suntri, P.* E. (?) large shrub or woody climber of the L. and M. H. F., from 2,000 to 5,000 ft. Fl. 4-5, fr. 12-3.

Capparis olacifolia, Hk. f. and T. *Naski, P.; Hais, P.; Jhenok-kúng, L.* E. (?) $\frac{10\text{-}15}{0\text{-}2+\frac{1}{2}\text{-}1}$ large shrub of the K. S. F. undergrowth in the Terai and by the banks of rivers, occasionally in L. H. F. Fl. 3-4, fr. 1-3 of succeeding year. Bark brown, rough. Wood white, soft, but close-grained. Flowers large, white, with yellow lip. Berries red or black.

Capparis viminea, Hk. f. and T. *Chinli, P.; Pundri-kúng, L.* Large shrub of L. H. F. from Terai up to 4,000 ft. Fl. 4, fr. 7.

Capparis (near floribunda). Large climbing shrub of M. H. F., about 4,000 ft. Fl. 6.

Roydsia suaveolens, Roxb. *Kasonli-lara, P.; Tunggor-rik, L.* Large climber of Terai and L. H. F. Fl. 3.

Cratœva religiosa, Forst. *Purbongnyok, L.* L. $\frac{30\text{-}40}{10\text{-}15+3\text{-}4}$ of the M. P. F. *d.*, K. S. F. and waste places in Terai and L. H. F. up to 2,000 ft. Fl. 3-4, fr. 7-8. Wood white, close-grained, not used.

VIOLACEÆ.

ALSODEIA BENGALENSIS, Wall. *Kalipat, P.* E. A large shrub or small tree of the L. H. F. damp valleys, *e.g.* near Sivoke.

BIXINEÆ.

BIXA ORELLANA, Linn. *Nali, P.* (?) I have seen this in gardens in Julpigori; it may probably be also found in the lower Terai. Cultivated for the "arnotto" dye which it produces.

GYNOCARDIA ODORATA, R. Br. *Kadoo, P.; Bandri, P.; Bandka, M.; Túk-kúng, L.* E. $\frac{30\text{-}50}{10\text{-}20+3\text{-}4}$ of the M. P. F. *w.* in the Terai and L. H. F. up to 4,000 ft. Fl. 5, fr. 11-1. Wood hard, red, used for many purposes; but it is not sufficiently common, and the tree scarcely straight enough for very general use. It is easily recognized by the hard round fruits which grow on the stem and main branches, and the pulp of which is used by the Lepchas to poison fish. The pulp is also eaten by Lepchas after boiling. The seeds give an oil, which does not seem to be used in Sikkim, though it is used in medicine in Bengal under the name "Chaulmoogra."

PITTOSPOREÆ.

PITTOSPORUM FLORIBUNDUM, W. & A. *Prongzam-kúng, L.* E. $\frac{10\text{-}20}{0\text{-}10+1\text{-}2}$, and perhaps occasionally larger, of the M. and U. H. F. from 5,000 to 8,000 ft. Fl. 5, fr. 11. Very common about Darjeeling and Dumsong.

POLYGALEÆ.

POLYGALA ARILLATA, Ham. *Karima, P.; Michepnor-kúng, L.* Large shrub of the M. and U. H. F. from 4,000 to 7,000 ft. Fl. 6, fr. 10. Flowers yellow. The root is said to be used as a "yeast" in the fermentation of "murwa" beer by the Bhutias. Wood used to procure fire by friction.

TAMARISCINEÆ.

TAMARIX DIOICA, Roxb. This is by no means uncommon in the Western Duars, and may probably be found in the Terai on the Mechi or Mahanadi rivers.

HYPERICINEÆ.

HYPERICUM (HOOKERIANUM, W. & A.). *Tumbomri, L.* Common shrub of the U. H. F., 3-6 ft. high. Exceedingly common in

Darjeeling, where it is often used for hedges. Fl. 6-7, fr. 11-12. Very handsome with its masses of bright yellow flowers. Bark brown. Wood hard, close-grained; polishes smooth.

NOTE.—There are two or three other species of a shrubby growth, chiefly from the Singalila range, but not well enough determined to mention. In Mr. C. B. Clarke's notes on a trip from Darjeeling to Tongloo, published in the Linnean Society's Journal for 1876, the species here given is called *H. Patulum, Thbg.*

GUTTIFERÆ.

GARCINIA STIPULATA, T. And. *Sanakadan-kúng, L.* E. $\frac{40\text{-}50}{10\text{-}30+3\text{-}5}$ of the L. H. F. up to 3,000 ft.; chiefly near streams. Very common in the valleys of the Tista and its affluents. Fl. 8-9, fr. 1-2. Fruit yellow, sometimes eaten by Lepchas. The tree and its fruit give a yellow gum, but it does not seem to be used.

NOTE.—I have found a small-leaved species growing 30 feet high in the Dalka Jhar; and *G. pedunculata, Roxb.*, is cultivated at Julpigori, and perhaps in the Terai.

CALOPHYLLUM POLYANTHUM, Wall. *Kironli, P.*; *Sunglyernyok, L.* E. $\frac{30\text{-}60}{15\text{-}30+4\text{-}10}$ (one specimen I measured at Latpanchor gave 11 ft. 8 in. girth, but this is unusual). Common large tree of the L. and M. H. F. from the Terai up to 5,000 ft. Fl. 5. Recognized by its opposite lanceolate leaves with prominent midrib and close parallel veins and white flowers. Wood said to be very strong and good.

TERNSTRÖMIACEÆ.

EURYA JAPONICA, Thunb. *Jhingni, P.*; *Tungchong-kúng, L.* E. $\frac{30\text{-}40}{5\text{-}15+2\text{-}4}$ of the M. H. F. from 3,000 to 6,000 ft. Fl. 8, fr. 11. Chiefly found in second-growth forest on old cultivations, mixed with *Schima Wallichii* and *Castanopsis Indica* and *tribuloides*. It is one of the trees which the Sikkim Bhutias in Kalimpúng leave in their fields to be yearly pollarded for manure. Coppices very well, and grows very quickly.

EURYA SYMPLOCINA, Bl. *Bara jhingni, P.*; *Kisri, P.*; *Flotung-chong-kúng, L.* E. $\frac{20\text{-}40}{5\text{-}15+2\text{-}3}$ of the M. and U. H. F. from 5,000 to 7,000 ft. Fl. 10, fr. 2. Bark brown, thin. Wood pink-white, with fine medullary rays, well marked annual rings, and numerous medullary spots; hard, easily worked, and does not warp much.

EURYA ACUMINATA, DC. *Sanu jhingni, P.*; *Flotungchong-kúng, L.* E. $\frac{15\text{-}20}{5\text{-}10+1\text{-}2}$. Small tree of the M. and U. H. F. from 5,000 to 8,000 ft. Fl. 3-4, fr. 6. Very common about Darjeeling. Bark brown, thin, smooth. Wood pink-white, resembling the former species but heavier and with fewer medullary spots. There is a variety with larger leaves and less pubescence, which I have found in the Dalka Jhar in the Terai.

ACTINIDIA CALLOSA, Ldl. *Tikiphal, P.; Tuksingrik, L.* Large climber of the M. H. F. about 5,000 ft. Fl. 5-6, fr. 11. Reaches 4 in. diameter. Bark corky, brown, rough. Wood brown, soft, open-grained, with no medullary rays and very large pores. Fruit edible, subacid, very pleasant.

ACTINIDIA STRIGOSA, Hk. f. and T. *Tikphal, P.; Tuksingrik, L.* L. large climber of the U. H. F. from 6,000 to 8,000 ft. Exceedingly common about the station of Darjeeling. Fl. 5, fr. 9. The fruit is edible, and is, I think, the best wild fruit in the district with the exception of the yellow raspberry, "*Rubus flavus.*" This creeper is almost yearly attacked by a caterpillar (about 1½ in. long, cream-coloured, with black and orange spots), which completely denudes it of its leaves.

NOTE.—A large climbing shrub, near *Actinidia callosa*, Ldl., and with strong hooked species is very common in the Dalka Jhar in the Terai.

SAURAUJA NEPALENSIS, DC. *Gogen, P.; Kasúr-kúng, L.* E. $\frac{20\text{-}30}{5\text{-}15+2\text{-}3}$ of the M. and U. H. F. from 4,000 to 7,000 ft. Fl. 1-5, fr. 9-10. Is chiefly common to the east of the Senchal range, rare to the west, as are all the species. Generally in second-growth forest, but also in old parts. Wood pink, with fine medullary rays, very soft, light, and liable to warp. Bark reddish brown, thin. Leaves used to feed cattle, for which purpose the tree is often regularly pollarded. Fruit eaten by Lepchas.

SAURAUJA GRIFFITHII, Dyer. *Gogen, P.; Hlosipha-kúng, L.* E. $\frac{15\text{-}20}{5\text{-}10+1\text{-}3}$ of the M. H. F. from 4,000 to 6,000 ft. Fl. 5-6, fr. 9-10. Very local. It is common on Sitong round Lamteng Pokri, but the only other place that I have ever seen it is below Chongtong, close to the Little Rangít Bridge, at 2,000 ft. A magnificent plant, with huge leaves of a bright green above and dense brown flocculent tomentum beneath and on the petioles and young shoots.

SAURAUJA FASCICULATA, Wall. *Saré gogen, P.; Sipha-kúng, L.* E. $\frac{10\text{-}15}{0\text{-}5+\frac{1}{2}\text{-}1}$ of the L. and M. H. F. from 2,000 ft. to 5,000 ft. Fl. 5. Has long leaves, densely ferruginous-tomentose beneath.

SAURAUJA PUNDUANA, Wall. *Rata gogen, P.; Sipha-kúng, L.* E. $\frac{15\text{-}25}{5\text{-}10+1\text{-}2}$ of the M. P. F. *w.* in Terai and L. H. F. up to 4,000 ft. Fl. 5. Resembles the last, but has larger leaves.

SAURAUJA ROXBURGHII, Wall. *Ouli gogen, P.; Dangsipha-kúng, L.* E. $\frac{20\text{-}30}{10\text{-}15+2\text{-}3}$ of the M. P. F. *w.* and banks of streams in Terai and L. H. F. valleys. Fl. 5. Fruit eaten by Lepchas.

SCHIMA WALLICHII, Choisy. *Chilauni, P.; Kúngsúng-kúng, L.; Sumbrong-kúng, L.* E. $\frac{60\text{-}100}{30\text{-}60+6\text{-}12}$. Very large tree of the S. F. (scarce) and M. P. F. *w.* in Terai, L. and M. H. F. up to 5,000 ft. Fl. 5, fr. 11-12. Bark black, with deep vertical clefts. In trees which have grown in the open it is smoother and of a dark-grey colour. Wood red or reddish brown, moderately hard, close-grained; used for every purpose of house-building. It does not warp much, but shrinks while seasoning, so that planking laid down green, as it usually is in the district, has to be often taken up again after a year and put down afresh. It is perhaps most common in the forests east of the Tista, and in the Murti-Jaldoka forest and the Lower Hills towards the Bhutan frontier it is the prevailing tree. Fine forests of it also exist in the Dalka Jhar, Bamunpokri upper plateau, and at Sukna. In the Hills it is generally smaller, and at Kalimpúng is generally preserved in cultivations for the branches, which are cut off and burnt for manure. It coppices well, and is profusely regenerated from seed, provided that sufficient light is obtainable for the seedlings.

CAMELLIA THEIFERA, Griff.; CAMELLIA THEA, Link. *Cha.* The tea plant. Cultivated in the Terai and up to 7,000 ft. almost. *C. theifera* is the "Assam" plant, and is cultivated in the Terai chiefly. *C. thea* is the "China" plant, cultivated on the hills and in the Terai; but lately "hybrid" varieties are the ones which have been most planted.

CAMELLIA DRUPIFERA, Lour. *Hingua, P.; Chashing, Bh. E.* $\frac{15\text{-}20}{0\text{-}3 + 1\text{-}2}$. A large much-branched shrub of the M. H. F. from 4,000 to 6,000 ft. Fl. 1. Much resembles the tea plant, but is more tomentose and has rounder leaves. Attempts have several times been made to make tea of the leaves, but without success. Wood hard and strong; prized for axe and hoe handles.

DIPTEROCARPEÆ.

SHOREA ROBUSTA, Gaertn. *Sâl. H. Sakwa M. P.; Teturl-kúng, L.* The Sâl tree. L. $\frac{80\text{-}150}{30\text{-}60+10\text{-}15}$. Found in S. F. in the Terai, in the L. H. F. on ridges up to 3,000 ft. from the Mechi river to the Chel, and in the inner valleys of the Tista, Great Rangít, and Rangpo rivers for a great distance, and to an elevation of 3,000 ft. Fl. 3-4, fr. 6. The most valuable tree in the district, the chief forest tree (and indeed almost the only gregarious one), and the chief source of revenue. (For description of the bark and wood c.f. *Brandis' Forest Flora,* and for details of its geographical distribution in the district and map reference may be made to the article "The Darjeeling Forests," at page 74 of Vol. I of the *Indian Forester.*) Used for building bridges, railway sleepers, &c., also for dug-out canoes. It gives a quantity of resin, which, happily, has not been much collected in the district. In some places in the Upper Tista forests large pieces, often nearly 30-40 cubic inches in size, are occasionally found in the ground at the foot of the trees. How they are produced is not known, but should be investigated. Specimens may be seen in the Conservator's office in Darjeeling and at the Economic Museum, Calcutta. Seedlings come up everywhere, but best in shade. When once, however, they are established, they require light, otherwise they are very liable to die off again.

MALVACEÆ.

KYDIA CALYCINA, Roxb. *Kubindé, P.; Mahow, M.; Sedangtaglar, L.* E. $\frac{30\text{-}40}{15\text{-}20+3\text{-}4}$ of the Sv. F. and M. P. F. *d.* in Terai and L. H. F. up to 2,000 ft. Fl. 9-10, fr. 1-2. Chiefly common in Savannahs. Bark grey-brown. Wood reddish, hard, close-grained, not used except for charcoal.

DICELLOSTYLES JUJUBIFOLIA, Bth. *Kubindé, P.; Dantaglar, L.* E. $\frac{20\text{-}30}{5\text{-}15+3\text{-}4}$ of the L. H. F. Fl. 1, fr. 3. Flowers white, in great abundance, furnished with big bracteoles, which remain with the fruit.

HIBISCUS SCANDENS, Roxb. Large climbing shrub of L. and M. H. F., from 1,000 to 4,000 ft. Fl. 10

NOTE.—Several species of *Hibiscus* and *Abutilon* are cultivated in gardens in the Terai and Lower Hills.

THESPESIA LAMPAS, Dalz. and Gibs. *Kaphalmúk, L.* Large shrub, with big yellow flowers. Common in L. H. F., *e.g.* about Pankabari. Fl. 8.

BOMBAX MALABARICUM, DC. *Semul, P.; Sungloo-kúng, L.* L. $\frac{80\text{-}100}{40\text{-}60+10\text{-}16}$ of all kinds of forest in Terai, but chiefly in Sv. F. and in L. H. F. up to 3,000 ft. Fl. 1-2, fr. 4-5. Bark grey-white, shining, soft. Stem covered when young with big conical prickles; when old, with small prickles. Branches in whorls. Stem very cylindrical, except at the base, where, when old, it forms large buttresses, often 4-6 ft. deep. The wood is light, soft, easily worked; it is in great demand for tea-boxes, and is used also for temporary "dug-out" canoes. A yellowish gum exudes from the bark. The fruit gives the "semul" cotton, of which large quantities are collected and sold for stuffing mattrasses, pillows, rezais, &c. The finest trees are found on the flats on the banks of rivers just within the hills, and on plateaux of rather damp forest, such as Bamunpokri; but it grows to a great size in Savannahs also, and appears not to suffer in the least from jungle fires after it has reached 30 ft. in height. It strikes very readily from cuttings even of big branches. Its growth from seed is also exceedingly quick.

STERCULIACEÆ.

STERCULIA VILLOSA, Roxb. *Udal, P.; Kunhlyem-kúng, L.* L. $\frac{40\text{-}60}{20\text{-}30+6\text{-}10}$ of the S. F. and M. P. F. *d.* in Terai, and L. H. F. up to 2,000 ft. Commonest in mixed forests, such as those on the Balasan, and between it and the Hurlia river, and in L. H. F. plateaux like Sukna or Bamunpokri. Fl. 1-2, fr. 6-7. The leaves fall in December and are not renewed till May. The bark is grey-brown, rather rough. The wood is light greyish brown, very light. It has numerous medullary rays, very large pores, and here and there concentric bands of a dark-brown colour. It is not generally used, though it has been tried for tea-boxes. If felled in the forest, it rots away in one year after felling; but sends up innumerable coppice shoots, of very strong and quick growth and difficult to extirpate. A copious white transparent gum exudes from wounds cut into the liber. The inner bark is extensively used for rope-making, and is very strong. It is stripped off young (very rarely old) trees; the innermost layers are rejected, as well as the outer ones; the rest are cut into strips and dried, and are made up into rope, which is used for making elephant dragging breast-bands as well as for other purposes.

STERCULIA COLORATA, Roxb. *Phirphiri, P.; Kanhlyem-kúng, L.* L. $\frac{30\text{-}40}{15\text{-}20+3\text{-}4}$ of the S. F. and M. P. F. *d.* in the Terai. Fl. 4. The flowers appear when the tree is leafless, and are of a brilliant scarlet colour. Wood soft, similar to that of *S. villosa.* It also gives a gum, but it is not used. The inner bark is also used for ropes, but is not so good as that of *S. villosa.*

STERCULIA COCCINEA, Roxb. *Katior-kúng, L.* Small tree of the L. H. F., and especially of the inner valleys up to 3,000 ft. Fl. 8. The Lepchas eat the flowers.

STERCULIA PALLENS (named by Kurz in H. B. C. Should it not be *fulgens, Wall.* ?). *Kaphal-kúng, L.* Large tree of the L. H. F. up to 3,000 ft. Flowers and fruits I have never seen. The roots of young trees have tubers, which are eaten by the Lepchas. Leaves soft, 3-lobed, of a yellowish tinge.

STERCULIA ALATA, Roxb. *Muslini, P.* Very large tree, up to 100 ft. high, of the L. H. F. Not very common, but I have several times seen it in the Tista valley. Leaves large, entire, cordate, 5-7 nerved, follicle big, woody.

REEVESIA PUBESCENS, Mast. *Kala boeri, P.* A tree of the L. and M. H. F. from 3,000 to 5,000 ft. Fl. 5, fr. 8. Not uncommon about Kurseong. Bark sometimes used to make ropes.

PTEROSPERMUM ACERIFOLIUM, Willd. *Hattipaila, P.* E. $\frac{40\text{-}60}{20\text{-}30+4\text{-}6}$ of the L. H. F. up to 4,000 ft. Fl. 5. Wood light red, rather close-grained, easily worked, takes a good polish, would probably be very good for furniture. This is a very handsome tree, with large flowers and large leaves, white tomentose beneath. The soft tomentum is used by Paharias to stop bleeding in wounds. The leaves are used as plates and for packing tobacco.

ERIOLÆNA, SP. A tree of the L. H. F., *e.g.* Bamunpokri upper plateau. Wood red-brown, hard, close-grained, much esteemed by Paharias.

ABROMA AUGUSTA, Linn. *Sanu-kapashi, P.* L. $\frac{10\text{-}15}{0\text{-}5+\frac{1}{2}\text{-}1}$. Small tree of L. and M. H. F. from Terai to 4,000 ft. Fl. 9, fr. 1. Probably introduced, but now common in the forests. The bark is said to give a good fibre, but it is rarely used. Seeds eaten.

BYTTNERIA PILOSA, Roxb. *Sali-lara, P.* A climbing shrub of the L. H. F. up to 4,000 ft. Fl. 5.

BYTTNERIA ASPERA, Coleb. *Nalgi*, P. A climbing shrub of the M. P. F. *w.* in Terai (common in the Dalka Jhar) and L. H. F. up to 4,000 ft. Fl. 5, fr. 8. Leaves given to cattle. The fruit is large, with strong stout spikes.

TILIACEÆ.

GREWIA EXCELSA, Vahl. Small tree of the inner valleys at 1,000 to 3,000 ft. Fl. 6, fr. 8-9.

GREWIA VESTITA, Wall. *Sealposra, P.; Kúnsúng-kúng, L.* L. (?) $\frac{20\text{-}40}{10\text{-}20+2\text{-}3}$ of the S. F., M. P. F. *d.* of Terai and L. H. F. up to 2,000 ft. Fl. 3-5. Very common. Wood grey-white, with numerous fine medullary rays and annual rings marked by a darker colour, strong and tough. Used by Nepalese occasionally for shingles. Leaves used to feed cattle.

GREWIA SAPIDA, Roxb. A small shrub springing up yearly from a perennial root-stock after the jungle fires in the Terai, S. F. and Sv. F. Fl. 3-4, bright yellow.

GREWIA SCABROPHYLLA, Roxb. Small shrub with large leaves and white flowers. Common in the lower S. F.. in the Terai, and in the grass lands between the "jhars." Fl. 6, fr. 11.

GREWIA MULTIFLORA, Juss. *Nilay, P.* E. $\frac{15\text{-}20}{5\text{-}10+1\text{-}2}$ of the M. P. F. *d.* and K. S. F. in Terai, but commonest along roadsides, in waste places near streams, and in thickets in the southern Terai, *e.g.* about Siliguri. Fl. 7-8, fr. 9-10. Wood grey-white, soft, much attacked by xylophages.

GREWIA LÆVIGATA, Vahl. *Dansagla, L.* E. $\frac{20\text{-}30}{5\text{-}10+1\text{-}3}$ of the Terai, K. S. F. and waste places, and L. H. F. up to 3,000 ft. Fl. 8, fr. 11. Wood white-grey, soft, useless. Recognized from the former, *G. multiflora*, by its much longer leaves and larger flowers; in other respects resembling it.

GREWIA POLYGAMA, Roxb. *Danbagla, L.* Small tree of the L. H. F. up to 3,000 ft. Fl. 5, fr. 7.

ECHINOCARPUS STERCULIACEUS, Bth. *Banj, P.* L. $\frac{60\text{-}100}{20\text{-}40+6\text{ }10}$. Very large tree of the M. P. F. *w.* in Terai and L. H. F. up to 2,000 feet. Fl. 2-3, fr. 11-12. Common round Sivoke. Stem cylindrical above, much and deeply buttressed below. Fruit big, armed with very long sharp spines.

ECHINOCARPUS TOMENTOSUS, Bth. *Kaktay, P.; Taksor-kúng, L.* Large fine tree of the L. and M. H. F. from 2,000 to 5,000 ft. Rather rare. Wood said to be good.

ECHINOCARPUS DASYCARPUS, Bth. *Gobria, P.* E. $\frac{60\text{-}100}{15\text{-}30+8\text{-}12}$ of the M. and U. H. F. from 5,000 to 7,000 ft. Fl. 10, fr. 11-12. One of the commonest, handsomest, and most valuable trees. Bark brown-grey, rough. Wood brown-white, used for house-building, tea-boxes, and to make charcoal, and has lately been in great demand. The tree often begins to branch very soon, and sometimes spreads out into many heads with drooping branches.

ELÆOCARPUS ROBUSTUS, Roxb. *Bepari, P.* E. $\frac{20\text{-}30}{5\text{-}15+3\text{-}5}$ of the M. P. F. *w.* in Terai Fl. 4-5. Common in the Dalka Jhar.

ELÆOCARPUS LANCEŒFOLIUS, Roxb. *Bhadras, P.; Batrachi, P.; Shepkyew-kúng, L.* E. $\frac{60\text{-}100}{20\text{-}40+8\text{-}12}$ of the U. H. F. from 6,000 to 8,000 ft. Fl. 8, fr. 3. Common in Darjeeling. Wood yellow-brown, rather soft, used for house-building, tea-boxes, charcoal, &c. Fruit eaten; it resembles a large olive in appearance, and also somewhat in flavour.

ELÆOCARPUS RUGOSUS, Roxb. *Nandiki, P.* E. large tree of the M. P. F. *w.* in Terai and L. H. F. Fl. 4.

NOTE.—There is another tree with a very big cylindrical stem in the U. H. F. with leaves almost entire and obovate, acuminate, smooth shining, and fruits like those of *E. lanceœfolius*, which is called *Bhadras* or *Geophal*: it may belong to this genus.

LINEÆ.

REINWARDTIA TRIGYNA, Planch. *Lalú, P.* A shrub common in M. H. F. from 3,000 to 5,000 ft., especially with a southerly aspect. Fl. bright yellow, 10-1.

REINWARDTIA TETRAGYNA, Planch. *Lalú, P.* Similar to, and found in the same places as, *R. trigyna.* Fl. 10.

MALPIGHIACEÆ.

HIPTAGE MADABLOTA, Gaertn. *Shempati, P.; Tungchirrik, L.* Large climber of the L. H. F. with handsome flowers. Fl. 3.

ASPIDOPTERYS ROXBURGHIANA, A. Juss. *Shubung-lara, P.; Munkuknyok, L.* Climber of the L. H. F. up to 3,000 ft. Fl. fr. 7-9.

ASPIDOPTERYS NUTANS, Hk. f. *Shubung-lara, P.; Simplútrik, L.* Climber of the Terai and L. H. F. up to 3,900 ft. Fl. fr. 7-9.

GERANIACEÆ.

AVERRHOA CARAMBOLA, Linn. *Kamaranga, H.* A small tree cultivated in the Terai for its fruit, large quantities of which are sold in the winter season.

RUTACEÆ.

EVODIA FRAXINIFOLIA, Hk. f. *Kanukpa, P. Kanú-kúng, L.* L. $\frac{20\text{-}30}{10\text{-}15+2\text{-}3}$ of the M. and U. H. F. from 4,000 to 7,000 ft., chiefly on cleared land. Fl. 5, fr. 8. Wood soft, not used except for temporary huts. Seeds eaten by hill-people.

ZANTHOXYLUM OVALIFOLIUM, Wt. Large shrub or small tree of the M. P. F. *w.* in Terai and L. H. F. valleys. Fl. 3-4, fr. 10.

Zanthoxylum alatum, Roxb. *Balay Timur, P.; Sungrú-kúng, L.* Large shrub or small tree of M. and U. H. F. from 4,000 to 7,000 ft. Fl. 10-11. Bark of stem covered with large conical prickles, that of the branches and the leaves covered with small sharp ones. The whole plant has a very unpleasant smell. Wood soft, yellowish white, close-grained.

Zanthoxylum acanthopodium, DC. *Bogay Timur, P.; Timbur, L.* E. $\frac{15\text{-}20}{0\text{-}5+1\text{-}2}$ of the M. and U. H. F. from 4,000 to 7,000 ft. Fl. fr. 9-11. Much resembles *Z. alatum*, but differs in the fruit and in the leaves being much smaller and closer; it has the same unpleasant smell. Wood yellowish white, rather soft.

Zanthoxylum oxyphyllum, Edgw. *Timur, P.; Siritakdangji, L.* Shrub, often climbing, of the U. H. F. Fl. 5. Flowers lilac, large.

Zanthoxylum Hamiltonianum, Wall. *Purpuray Timur, P.* A large climbing shrub of the M. and U. H. F. Fl. 5, fr. 10.

Toddalia aculeata, Pers. *Meinkara, P.; Saphiji-rik, L.* Large prickly climbing shrub of the M. and U. H. F., from 3,000 to 7,000 ft. Fl. 2, fr. 12. Wood yellow, hard, close-grained. Fruit yellow, like a little orange, eaten by Lepchas and Paharias.

Acronychia laurifolia, Bl. *Paowlay, P.* E. $\frac{15\text{-}25}{5\text{-}10+2\text{-}3}$ of the M. P. F. *w.* in Terai, L. and M. H. F., up to 4,000 ft. Fl. fr. 12.

Skimmia Laureola, Hook. f. *Chumlani, P.; Timbernyok, L.* Large shrub of M. and U. H. F. from 5,000 to 9,000 ft. Fl. 5, fr. 11. Bark greenish brown, smooth. Wood white, very hard, close-grained, takes a good polish. Medullary rays very numerous and fine. Pores small, arranged in curious small zigzag lines. Used to make hoe and axe handles.

Glycosmis pentaphylla, Corréa. Large shrub or small tree of the M. P. F. *w.* and L. H. F. up to 4,000 ft. Fl. 3. (There are several varieties of this, which have been separated and described by S. Kurz in the *Journal of Botany* for February 1876.)

Micromelum pubescens, Bl. *Lasmani, P.; Kumbrong-kúng, L.* E. $\frac{15\text{-}20}{0\text{-}5+1\text{-}2}$ of the M. P. F. *w.* in Terai and L. H. F. up to 3,000 ft. Chiefly in valleys. Fl. 12, fr. 4.

Murraya exotica, Linn. *Simali, P.; Shitzem-kúng, L.* E. $\frac{10\text{-}15}{0\text{-}3+\frac{1}{2}\text{-}1}$ of the M. P. F. *w.* in Terai and L. H. F. up to 3,000 ft. Common about Sivoke and Dalingkot, but rare west of the Balasan. Fl. 3-8, fr. 10-2. Wood white, very hard, close-grained, somewhat resembling box-wood. Often found in gardens. Flowers white, very sweet-scented.

Murraya Königii, Spreng. Small tree of the Terai forests, L. and M. H. F. up to 6,000 ft. Fl. 3, fr. 7.

Clausena excavata, Burm. A small plant, which comes up in the Terai from a perennial root-stock at all seasons of the year, chiefly in spring. (In the *Flora Indica* it is described as a tree, but it rarely reaches more than 2 ft. as far as I have seen.)

Clausena Willdenovii, W. & A. *Madanay, P.; Terhilnyok, L.*; *Sidemnyok, L.* Small tree of the M. and U. H. F. from 3,000 to 6,000 ft. Fl. 4-5, fr. 7.

Paramignya monophylla, Wt. *Natkanta, P.; Jhunok-kúng, L.* Large shrub, common in the L. H. F. valleys and up to 3,000 ft. Fl. 3. Wood white, hard, close-grained, heavy, but small. Thorny shrub, much resembling the lime.

Citrus medica, Linn. *Kachi-kúng, L.* Different kinds:—*Nimbor, P.*; *Naitijemi, P.*; *Bimir, P.* The citron and lime. Cultivated in the Terai and Hills, even in Darjeeling, at 7,000 ft.

Citrus Aurantium, Linn. *Naringi*; *Kamla*; *Suntala, P.; Silumkúng, L.* The orange. Cultivated in the inner ranges, giving very good fruit. Large quantities are exported from Sikkim every year to the plains. A few fine trees may be seen near Kalimpúng and at Gielle.

Citrus decumana, Linn. *Kaljemi, P.*; *Lumbo-kúng, L.* The pumelo. Cultivated in the Terai and Lower Hills.

Feronia Elephantum, Corréa. I have seen this once or twice in cultivation in the Terai.

Ægle Marmelos, Corréa. *Bael, P.* The bael tree. Cultivated in the Terai.

SIMARUBEÆ.

Picrasma javanica, Bl. *Tungjir-kúng, L.* Small tree of the inner valleys in the Hills. Fl. 4-5.

Brucea mollis, Wall. A shrub of the L. H. F. Not common. Fl. 4.

OCHNACEÆ.

Ochna pumila, Ham. A small under-shrub of the S. F. and Sv. F. in the Terai, coming up in spring, and especially after jungle fires, from a perennial root-stock. Fl. 3, large, yellow, handsome.

BURSERACEÆ.

Garuga pinnata, Roxb. *Dabdabbi, P.; Gia. M.; Maldit-kúng, L.* L. $\frac{60\text{-}80}{30\text{-}40+4\text{-}6}$ of the S. F., Sv. F., M. P. F. *d.* in Terai and L. H. F. up to 3,000 ft. Fl. 4, fr. 8. Wood greyish white, soft, not used, though it would probably do for tea-boxes. It gives a clear gum of little or no value. The leaves are much lopped for fodder. In the Terai forests it is generally small, except in the dry M. P. F., but in the Hills it grows to a very large size.

Canarium Bengalense, Roxb. *Goguldhup, P.*; *Narockpa, L.* E. $\frac{80\text{-}150}{50\text{-}70+4\text{-}6}$ of the L. H. F. and up to 3,000 ft. Bark hard, thin, rough, with horizontal wrinkles. Wood white, open-grained, soft, light, with large medullary rays. Much in request for tea-boxes and shingles, but it rots away very readily, and is hardly as good as "semul." It gives a resin, which is used by Lepchas to burn as incense. A magnificent tree, with a very tall, almost perfectly cylindrical, stem. It has been a good deal cut out, but fine specimens may still be seen, *e.g.* on the cart road near Tindharia and in the Rangbi Valley.

MELIACEÆ.

MUNRONIA WALLICHII, Wight. A shrub of the L. H. F., with pretty pink flowers. Fl. 4.

MELIA AZEDARACH, Linn. *Bukayun, H.; Bukainú, P.* Cultivated near villages in the Terai, and often found, apparently wild, on sites of old villages in the forest. Fl. 12.

(MELIA COMPOSITA, Willd.) *Labshi, P.; Silot-kúng, L.* A large tree of the L. and M. H. F. up to 6,000 ft. It has a red wood, with the appearance and odour of Toon. Fruit eaten.

DYSOXYLUM BINECTARIFERUM, Hook. *f. Katongzu, L.* Large tree of the L. H. F. Fr. 12. Wood red, hard, and close-grained. Fruit large, four-celled, red.

DYSOXYLUM HAMILTONII, Hiern. *Bauriphal, P.* Large tree of the M. P. F. *w.* in Terai and L. H. F. Fr. 1. Fruit yellow.

DYSOXYLUM ALLIACEUM, Bl. *Chalégachh, P.; Silhokmongú, P.* Tree of the M. P. F. *w.* in Terai and L. H. F. Fl. 12, with a very strong alliaceous odour.

AGLAIA EDULIS, A. Gray. *Lati mahwa, P.; Sinakadang-kúng, L.* Tree of the L. H. F. up to 3,000 ft. Fl. 8, fr. 4. Fruit edible.

AMOORA ROHITUKA, W. & A. *Bandriphal, P.; Tangarook-kúng, L.* E. $\frac{20\text{-}30}{10\text{-}15+2\text{-}3}$ of the M. P. F. *w.* in Terai and L. and M. H. F., up to 6,000 ft. Common in second-growth forest, about 5,000 ft. Fl. 4, fr. 12. Wood pink, close-grained, rather soft. Fruit yellow.

AMOORA DECANDRA, Hiern. *Tangarook-kúng, L.* Tree of the L. and M. H. F. from 2,000 to 6,000 ft. Fl. 5-6.

HEYNEA TRIJUGA, Roxb. *Akhaterwa, P.* L. $\frac{20\text{-}40}{15\text{-}20+3\text{-}4}$ of the S. F. and M. P. F. *w.* in Terai and L. H. F. up to 4,000 ft. Fl. 4, fr. 8. The seeds give an oil, used for burning by Nepalese.

CEDRELA TOONA, Roxb. *Tuni, P.; Simal-kúng, L.* There seem certainly to me to be three distinct varieties under this, though in the *Flora Indica* and in *Brandis' Forest Flora* they are all put under one head. It will consequently be better to describe them separately, especially as the tree is now being extensively grown both by Government and by planters, and as great care has to be taken to procure the seed of the variety most suited to the locality of the plantation.

No. 1.—*Bobich, P.* L. $\frac{30\text{-}50}{10\text{-}25+4\text{-}5}$ of the M. P. F. *d.* and K. S. F. Fl. 4, fr. 6. Bark brown or greyish brown, smooth, not exfoliating. Wood pink or pinkish white, with a strong odour, soft, open-grained, light, said not to be durable. This variety is common in the forests on the banks of the Balasan, Manjha, and Mechi rivers. It is very extensively lopped for fodder—a practice which generally causes the inside of the tree to decay quickly.

No. 2.—*Tuni*, *P*. E. (?) $\frac{40\text{-}60}{20\text{-}30+4\text{-}6}$ of the L. H. F., up to 4,000 ft. Fl. 10-11, fr. 2-3. Bark dark brown, rough, but not exfoliating in scales. Wood pink or red, turning darker when cut up, rather soft, with a strong odour, but durable. This is probably the best kind. It is the variety which is being grown at Bamunpokri plantation. If not grown closely, it is very liable to begin to branch at an early age, and consequently to produce only a small quantity of timber big enough for sawing up. It is much exposed to the attacks of a beetle, the larva of which yearly eats out the inside pith from young trees, causing the tops to die off.

No. 3.—*Lapshi*, *P*. E. $\frac{80\text{-}120}{40\text{-}60+10\text{-}20}$ of the M. and U. H. F. from 5,000 to 7,000 ft. Fl. 7, fr. 11-12. Bark brown or reddish brown, peeling off in long flakes, giving the stem a shaggy appearance. Wood dark pink, turning dark red after exposure, soft, open-grained, but durable; has a fainter odour than Nos. 1 and 2. Leaves much bigger and longer. This is the kind which is being grown in Rungyrúm plantation. Formerly it must have been exceedingly common in the M. H. F. and lower part of the U. H. F., to judge by the immense amount of old toon timber, some of it of very large size, lying on the ground at an altitude of 4,000 to 6,000 ft. everywhere where Lepchas have been cultivating. A few fine trees may still be seen in the Tukdah Reserve, and it is common all over the Dumsong forests. It is very much lopped to feed cattle.

The wood of all three varieties is much the same, and used for all purposes—house-building, shingles (big ones for Bhutia houses), tea-boxes, chairs, tables, &c. It is hollowed into rice-pounders by the Lepchas. It is used by the Bhutias for wood-carving work, and is their favourite wood for all purposes of house-building and furniture. It is very easily grown from seed, and also coppices well; but plantations should be grown closely, say at most 5 ft. apart, to prevent too early branching. As for the best age for transplanting, opinions differ very much; experience at Bamunpokri and Rungyrúm has shown that plants pricked out once in the nurseries and transplanted when from one year to eighteen months old have succeeded best, but many persons are of opinion that the best time is when from three to six months old only.

NOTE.—The mahogany, *Swietenia Mahogani*, L., was once planted on a large area near Sukna, but afterwards all the plants died, probably from fire. It has been tried at Bamunpokri; but although it grew well at first, it almost invariably died when about 4-6 ft. high. Good specimens may be seen on the roadside near Titalya; but, owing to their being in the open, they are short and much branched.

OLACINEÆ.

ERYTHROPALUM SCANDENS, Bl. *Suntúngrúngrik, L.* Climbing shrub of the L. H. F. valleys. Fl. 5.

LEPIONURUS OBLONGIFOLIUS, Mast. Small tree of the L. H. F. Fl. 4, fr. 7.

NATSIATUM HERPETICUM, Ham. *Sungoo-rik, L.* A thin, wiry, climbing shrub of the K. S. F. and banks of streams in Terai and along river-beds in the L. Hills. Fl. 12-1.

DAPHNIPHYLLOPSIS CAPITATA, Kurz. *Kalay, P.*; *Chilauni, P.* (?); *Tumbrúng-kúng, L.* E. $\frac{60\text{-}80}{20\text{-}30+6\text{-}8}$ of the M. and U. H. F. from 5,000 to 7,000 ft. Common in the forests of Senchul and Mahalderam, and at Dumsong. Fl. ?, fr. 10-11. Wood yellow-white, rather hard, good, used for house-building about Darjeeling and Kurseong.

ILICINEÆ.

ILEX INSIGNIS, Hk. f. *Lasuni, P.* (?) E. $\frac{20\text{-}25}{5\text{-}15+2\text{-}3}$. Common in the station of Darjeeling, and, though rather rarer, in the forests round from 6,000 to 8,000 ft. Fl. 2-3, fr. 11-12. A very pretty tree, with large prickly leaves and bright red berries.

ILEX DIPYRENA, Wall. E. $\frac{30\text{-}40}{15\text{-}20+3\text{-}4}$ of the U. H. F. from 7,000 to 9,000 ft. Found at Rungbool and on Senchal.

ILEX GODAYAM, Colebr. E. $\frac{40\text{-}50}{20\text{-}25+3\text{-}4}$ of the M. P. F. in the Terai, *e.g.* in the lower portion of the Dalka Jhar, about Gundha Haga. Fl. 4.

CELASTRINEÆ.

EVONYMUS FRIGIDUS, Wall. Straggling shrub of the U. H. F. and R. F. from 7,000 to 10,000 ft. Fl. 5, fr. 8-10. A variety with very long leaves is common about Tongloo.

EVONYMUS ECHINATUS, Wall. *Sanu kimú, P.* Shrub, often epiphytic, of the U. H. F. Common about Darjeeling. Fl. 5, fr. 8.

EVONYMUS THEÆFOLIUS, Wall. Shrub, common about Darjeeling. Fl. .

MICROTROPIS DISCOLOR, Wall. *Suglim-kúng, L.* Large shrub or small tree of the L. and M. H. F. from the Terai to 6,000 ft. Fl. 11, fr. 1.

CELASTRUS PANICULATA, Willd. *Ruglimrik, L.* Large climbing shrub of the Terai, L. and M. H. F. up to 6,000 ft. Fl. 7, fr. 1-2. Bark yellow, corky. Wood yellow-pink, rather curious, consisting of broad medullary rays separated by thin layers of tissue. Annual layers marked by a ring of large sized vessels. It reaches 1-2 ft. in girth.

CELASTRUS STYLOSA, Wall. *Sukurruglim-rik, L.* Large climbing shrub of the U. H. F. from 6,000 to 8,000 ft. Very common in Darjeeling. Fl. 5, fr. 1-2. Bark yellow, corky. Wood like that of *C. paniculata*.

CELASTRUS MONOSPERMA, Roxb. *Tumbrúng-rik, L.* Large climbing or straggling shrub of the M. H. F. from 3,000 to 6,000 ft. Fl. 5, fr. 8-9.

GYMNOSPORIA THOMSONI, Kurz. *Phugong-kúng, L.* Large shrub of the M. and U. H. F. from 4,000 to 7,000 ft. Fl. 5-6, fr. 1-2.

ELÆODENDRON ROXBURGHII, W. & A. *Chikyeng-kúng, L.* L. $\frac{30\text{-}40}{15\text{-}20+3\text{-}5}$ of the L. H. F. up to 2,000 ft. Not very common. Fl. 7, fr. 12. Bark white-grey, peeling off, when dry, in small horizontal flakes. Wood pinkish white, with numerous small pores arranged very prettily in concentric lines, hard, close-grained, seasons very well, works easily, and takes a good polish.

RHAMNEÆ.

ZIZYPHUS JUJUBA, Lamk. *Baer, H. P.* L. $\frac{10\text{-}20}{0\text{-}10+1\text{-}4}$. Found growing in dense thickets over the S. Terai at and below Siliguri. Very rare in the forests, and then probably only on the sites of old villages. Often cultivated, and then reaches a pretty large size. Berries eaten. Fl. 8, fr. 12-1.

ZIZYPHUS RUGOSA, Lam. *Rukh Baer, P.* L. $\frac{10\text{-}20}{0\text{-}10+2\text{-}3}$, of the S. F., Sv. F., and M. P. F. *d.* in Terai and L. H. F. up to 2,000 ft. Fl. 4, fr. 9-10. Bark black-brown, peeling off in small rectangular scales. Wood red or reddish brown, hard, heavy, but warps very badly; is much attacked by insects even when green.

NOTE.—There are one or two other species, chiefly small and of the lower Terai.

BERCHEMIA FLORIBUNDA, Wall. *Chiaduk, P.; Rungyeong-rik, L.* Large climber of the M. H. F. from 4,000 to 6,000 ft. Fl. 12, fr. 3. Bark outside grey-white; deeply cleft, rough, falls off, leaving a purple-coloured inner bark exposed. Wood yellow, pretty, with numerous medullary rays and large pores; rather heavy, hard. The young leaves are poisonous to cattle.

RHAMNUS NEPALENSIS, Wall. *Achal, P.* Large shrub of L. H. F. up to 3,000 ft. Fl. ?, fr. 11-12.

RHAMNUS VIRGATUS, Roxb. Shrub of the M. and U. H. F., chiefly about 5,000 ft. Fl. 5-6, fr. 9.

GOUANIA LEPTOSTACHYA, DC. *Batwasi, P.; Tungcheongmonrik, L.* Climbing shrub of L. and M. H. F. from the Terai up to 6,000 ft. Fl. 8, fr. 12. The leaves are used by Lepchas to make poultices for sores.

AMPELIDEÆ.

VITIS DISCOLOR, Dalz. *Sanu Pureni, P.* Climber of the L. H. F. from 1,000 to 4,000 ft. Fl. 9, fr. 10. Has very handsome, variegated leaves, and red branches and flowers. Often cultivated in gardens.

VITIS GLAUCA, W. and A. *Pureni, P.*; *Kungchen-rik, L.* Climber of the M. P. F. in the Terai and L. H. F. up to 2,000 ft. Fl. 8, fr. 9-10. Leaves cordate. Stems glaucous.

VITIS REPANDA, W. and A. *Pani-lara, P.*; *Vhym-rik, L.* Large climber of the S. F., M. P. F. *d.* and L. H. F. ridges, climbing over the loftiest trees. Fl. 5. Bark brown, corky. Wood very soft, fibrous, holds a large quantity of water. Leaves large, cordate.

VITIS ADNATA, Wall. *Pani-lara, P.*; *Kungchen-rik, L.* A climber of the Terai and L. H. F. up to 3,000 ft. Fl. fr. 8-12. Leaves cordate, eaten by Lepchas.

VITIS BARBATA, Wall. Climber of the Terai. Fl. 5. Stems very hairy.

VITIS LANATA, Roxb. *Jarila-lara, P.*; *Mikrúm-rik, L.* Climbing shrub of the Terai and L. H. F. up to 3,000 ft. Fl. 4, fr. 6. Bark hard, peeling off in long strips. Wood with fine medullary rays and large pores, rather heavier than that of most kinds. Fruit eaten by Lepchas.

VITIS VINIFERA, Linn. The Vine. Cultivated occasionally by planters in the Terai, where it yields a fair description of fruit.

VITIS CARNOSA, Wall. *Jarila-lara, P.*; *Takbli-rik, L.* Climber of the L. Hills, up to 2,000 ft. Leaves trifoliolate. Fl. 8.

VITIS BRACTEOLATA, Wall. Climber of the M. P. F. *w.* in Terai. Fl. 3. Leaves trifoliolate.

VITIS HIMALAYANA, Brandis. *Bara churcheri, P.*; *Hlotagbret, L.* A very large climber of the U. H. F. from 5,000 to 10,000 ft., climbing over the highest trees. Fl. 5-6, fr. 9. Leaves trifoliolate, wrinkled.

VITIS ELONGATA, Wall. A large climber of the swampy parts of the M. P. F. *w.* in Terai and L. H. F. valleys up to 4,000 ft. Stem rather flattened; younger portions green. Leaves 5-foliolate, pedate.

VITIS CAPRIOLATA, Don. *Churcheri, P.* A large climber of the U. H. F. from 6,000 to 8,000 ft., climbing over trees and rocks. Common in Darjeeling. Fl. 5, fr. 10. Very pretty, with small pedate, 5-foliolate leaves.

VITIS TERNIFOLIA, W. and A. *Tukbrinyok, L.* Climber of the L. H. F. valleys and up to 4,000 ft. Leaves pedate, 5-foliolate, much serrated.

VITIS LANCEOLARIA, Roxb. *Tukbret-rik, L.* Climber of the L. H. F. up to 4,000 ft. Fr. 8. Leaves fleshy, pedate, 5-foliolate. Fruit big, rather dry.

VITIS RUMICISPERMA, Lawson. *Tungroot-rik, L.* Large climber of the M. and U. H. F. from 5,000 to 7,000 ft. Fl. 5, fr. 9. Fruit eaten. Attempts have been made by Darjeeling residents to make wine of it, but with indifferent success. When ripe it is not unpleasant to eat. Leaves 5-foliolate.

VITIS PEDATA, Vahl. *Tungrootrikup, L.* Climber of the Terai and L. H. F. up to 3,000 ft. Fl. fr. 4-5. Leaves pubescent, 5-foliolate.

NOTE.—There are several other species, which may be inserted hereafter. They are none of them important.

LEEA MACROPHYLLA, Roxb. *Bulyettrc, P.; Dampantóm-kúng, L.* Large herbaceous shrub of the S. F. and Sv. F. in Terai. Fl. 7-8. Leaves simple, very large, cordate, white beneath. The Paharias use the seeds of this to hang round children's necks as a kind of charm to drive away pains in the stomach.

LEEA ALATA, Edgw. *Lal galeni, P.; Tsemangri, P.; Kantóm-nok, L.* Herbaceous shrub of the S. F. and Sv. F. in Terai. Fl. 7, fr. 10. Flower and fruit scarlet. Leaflets rather long, narrow.

LEEA CRISPA, Willd. *Phekri galeni, P.; Pantóm, L.* Large herbaceous shrub of the S. F. and Sv. F. in Terai and dry L. H. F. Fl. 6, fr. 10. Leaves ovate-oblong, deeply serrate. Stems and branches with crisped wings.

LEEA LŒTA, Wall. *Lal galeni, P.; Pantóm. L.* Large herbaceous shrub of the M. P. F. *w.* in Terai and L. H. F. valleys. Fl. 6, fr. 9. Flowers scarlet. Leaves rather thin, long, acuminate.

LEEA ASPERA, Wall. *Galeni, P.; Pantóm, L.* Large herbaceous shrub of the L. H. F. up to 3,000 feet. Fl. 5. white; fr. 6-7, blue. Leaves rough, with rows of short bristles between the veins.

LEEA HIRTA, Roxb. *Galeni, P.; Mangú pantu-kúng, L.* Large shrub of the L. H. F. valleys up to 2,000 ft. Fl. 6, fr. 10, yellow or black. Leaves large, scabrous.

LEEA ROBUSTA, Roxb. *Galeni, P.; Pantóm, L.* Large shrub, often 10-12 ft. high, of Terai and L. H. F. up to 4,000 ft. Common on dry ridges in the L. Hills under Sâl. Fl. 4-5, fr. 7-9. Leaves very large, with big red bracts. Bark grey, with brown vertical lines. Stem fluted. Pith very large, grooved. Wood hard, with broad medullary rays.

LEEA SUMATRANA, Kurz. *Galeni, P.; Sirispanterr-kúng, L.* Large shrub of the Terai and L. H. F. up to 3,000 ft Fl. 4-5, with long lanceolate bracts and numerous bracteoles. Leaves rough, pubescent, very long, acuminate.

LEEA (GIGANTEA, Griff). *Galeni, P.* E. $\frac{15-25}{5-10+\frac{1}{2}-1}$ of the L. H. F. up to 3,000 ft. Found chiefly in valleys. Above Sivoke in the Tista valley many fine specimens may be seen along the road. Fl. ?, fr. 12, black. Leaflets many, small.

LEEA SAMBUCINA, Willd. *Galeni, P.; Pantóm, L.* Large shrub of the L. H. F. up to 4,000 feet. Fl. fr. 6-9. Fruit many-seeded, blue, eaten. Leaves rather small, generally crenate serrate.

SAPINDACEÆ.

Allophylus Zeylanicus, Linn. *Kautiernyok, L.* Shrub of the L. H. F. valleys, up to 3,000 ft. This is the var. *grandifolia.* Fl. 7-8, fr. 9-10.

Æsculus Punduana, Wall. *Cherinangri, P.* L. $\frac{40\text{-}50}{20\text{-}30+6\text{-}8}$ of the L. H. F. valleys up to 4,000 and M. P. F. *w.* in Terai. (Not found by me in the Darjeeling district, but I have found it at Rajbatkowa, in the Western Duars. It is here entered as the Flora Indica, and Dr. Brandis gives Sikkim as a locality.) Fl. 3.

Sapindus attenuatus, Wall. *Achatta. P.*; *Sirhootúngchir, L.* E. $\frac{10\text{-}13}{1\text{-}5+\frac{1}{4}\text{-}\frac{1}{2}}$. Shrub or small tree of the S. F. and M. P. F. *w.* in Terai and L. H. F up to 3,000 ft. Fl 2-3., fr. 4-5. It is easily recognized by the dark red flowers and red bi-lobed ellipsodial fruit.

Acer oblongum, Wall. L. $\frac{50\text{-}60}{30\text{-}40+5\text{-}7}$ of the M. H. F. about 4,000 to 5,000 feet. Fl. 11, fr. 1-2. Recognized by the long petioles and entire small oblong leaves, which are glaucous beneath.

Acer lævigatum, Wall. *Thali kabashi, P.*; *Tungnyok-kúng. L.* L. $\frac{60\text{-}80}{40\text{-}60+8\text{-}12}$ of the M. and U. H. F. from 5,000 to 9,000 ft. Recognized by small entire lanceolate leaves, not glaucous beneath. Fl. 3-4, fr. 5-6.

Acer Hookeri, Miq. *Lal kabashi, P.*; *Palé-kúng, L.* L. $\frac{20\text{-}30}{10\text{-}15+3\text{-}4}$ of the U. H. F. from 7,000 to 10,000 feet. Very common round Darjeeling and on Tongloo, often seen growing from seed deposited in the fork of another tree, and so apparently, though not really, epiphytic. Easily recognized by the red branches and petioles and generally reddish, cordate, very sharply serrate and occasionally, though rarely, 3-lobed leaves. Bark brown, cracked rather deeply. Wood light brown, soft, with a few medullary spots, easily worked.

Acer Sikkimense, Miq. *Palegnyok, L.* L. $\frac{20\text{-}30}{10\text{-}15+3\text{-}4}$ of the U. H. F. especially in open spaces like round Darjeeling. Fl. 4-5, fr. 5 6. It is easily distinguished by its leaves, which are serrate when young and entire when old. They are long-acuminate, cordate, of a bright green on both sides, and have hairs on the veins of the upper surface and a white tuft in the axil beneath when young. The inflorescence is spicate.

Acer caudatum, Wall. *Kabashi, P.*; *Yalishin, Bh.* L. $\frac{50\text{-}60}{20\text{-}30+6\text{-}8}$ of the R. F. from 8,000 to 11,000 ft. Fl. 3-4, fr. 10-11. Easily distinguished by sharp, 5-lobed, serrate leaves, with red branches and petioles, and by the bright red fruits with much diverging wings.

Acer Thomsoni, Miq. *Kabashi, P.* L. $\frac{60\text{-}90}{30\text{-}40+6\text{-}10}$. M. H. F. up to 6,000 feet. Most common at about 4,000 to 5,000 feet, *e.g.* in the forests round Paiengaon, Dumsong. Wood white, soft.

Recognized by the large plane-like leaves and large reddish fruit. Fl. 11-12, fr. 9-10. Wood white, soft. (In the *Flora Indica* the range is given as 7,000 to 9,000 ft., but I have never seen it above 6,000 ft., and it is very common in forests at about 5,000 feet. Can it be *A. Thomsoni*?)

Acer Campbellii, Hk. f. and T. *Kabashi, P.*; *Daom-kúng, L.*; *Yatli-kúng, L.* L. $\frac{80\text{-}100}{40\text{-}60+10\text{-}15}$. U. H. F. from 7,000 to 10,000 ft. Very common. Fl. 4-5, fr. 9-10. Wood light, brownish white, even-grained, works well, is much used for planking in native houses, tea-boxes, &c. The seedlings come up very freely self-sown, provided there is not much shade. It is recognized by the deeply 5-cut leaves and their bright light-green colour and reddish petioles.

Dobinœa vulgaris, Ham. *Samli, P.* Shrub of the M. H. F. from 4,000 to 6,000 ft. Fl. 8-9, fr. 10-11.

Dodonœa viscosa, Linn. A shrub occasionally used to make hedges in the Terai, but not common.

Turpinia pomifera, DC. *Nagpat, P.*; *Singnok-kúng, L.* E. $\frac{30\text{-}40}{15\text{-}20+3\text{-}4}$ of the M. P. F. *w.* in Terai and L. H. F. up to 3,000 ft. Fl. 3, fr. 9. Wood grey, rather heavy, close-grained, not used. Flowers in dense terminal panicles. Leaves pinnate, rather large.

Turpinia Nepalensis, Wall. *Thali, P.*; *Murgut-kúng, L.* E. $\frac{30\text{-}40}{20\text{-}25+3\text{-}4}$ of the M. and U. H. F. from 4,000 to 7,000 ft. Fl. 4, fr. 10. Wood white, rather hard. Has smaller leaves and flowers and a straighter growth than the former. Its leaves are much lopped to feed cattle.

SABIACEÆ.

Sabia leptandra, Hk. f. and T. *Simali-lara, P.*; *Payong-rik, L.* Straggling or climbing shrub of the M. and U. H. F. from 4,000 to 7,000 ft. Fl. 10-11, fr. 12.

Sabia parviflora, Wall. *Simali-lara, P.*; *Payong-rik, L.* Climbing shrub of the M. H. F. about 4,000 to 5,000 ft. Fl. 3.

Sabia paniculata, Edgw. *Kali-lara, P.* A climbing shrub of the L. H. F. Fl. 1. A fine specimen grows just over the spring at Bamunpokri, and it may also be found in the Bamunjhora; I have seen it nowhere else.

Sabia limoniacea, Wall. Climbing shrub of the U. H. F.

Meliosma dilleniœfolia, Wall. *Siamunú, P.* Tree of the M. and U. H. F. from 5,000 to 8,000 ft. Fr. 9.

Meliosma simplicifolia, Roxb. *Kosrú, P.*; *Hingman-kúng, L.* E. $\frac{30\text{-}40}{16\text{-}20+3\text{-}4}$. Very common in the M. P. F. *w.* in Terai and L. H. F. valleys. Fl 12-2, fr 5. Wood reddish brown, with numerous medullary rays, rather hard, but warps much, and is much attacked by xylophages.

Meliosma pinnata, Roxb. *Bolay, P.* Large tree of the L. H. F. up to 3,000 ft. Fr. 9.

MELIOSMA WALLICHII, Planch. *Nunewalai, P.*; *Himan-kúng, L.* Large tree of the M. and U. H. F. from 5,000 to 8,000 ft. Fl. 6-7. Common round Darjeeling.

ANACARDIACEÆ.

RHUS SEMIALATA, Murray. *Bhagmili, P.*; *Takhril-kúng, L.* L. $\frac{20\text{-}30}{10\text{-}15+2\text{-}3}$ of the L. and M. H. F. from 2,000 to 6,000 ft. Fl. 9-10, fr. 10-11. Very common in old Lepcha cultivations, *e.g.* in the Pashok forest above the Great Rangít, where it has come up in very great profusion. Bark grey, with numerous reddish brown lenticels. Sapwood white, heartwood grey-white, with a slight bluish tinge, soft, light. The seeds are eaten by Paharias and Lepchas. They are also made into a wax, *Omlu, P.*

RHUS ACUMINATA, DC. *Raniwalai, P.*; *Serhnyok, L.* L. $\frac{16\text{-}20}{5\text{-}10+1\text{-}2}$ of the U. H. F. especially in cleared ground, as about the station of Darjeeling. Fl. 5, fr. 10. Very handsome at any time, but especially in autumn, when its leaves turn to different shades, from bright orange to deep scarlet. The juice causes blisters.

RHUS INSIGNIS, Hk. f *Kagphulai, P.*; *Serh-kúng, L.* L. A tree of the U. H. F. from 6,000 to 8,000 ft., often growing to 50 ft. high, with a girth of 4-5 ft. Fl. 7, fr. 12 One of the handsomest trees in the district. Common in Darjeeling. The juice raises blisters.

MANGIFERA INDICA, Linn. *Am. H.*; *Lowri Am., P.*; *Ambhi, L.* The mango tree. Cultivated everywhere in the Terai and Lower Hills up to a considerable elevation; its fruit, however, is generally very poor. On one or two tea plantations the manager has grown it very successfully from good grafts, but the ordinary village mango is not worth eating.

MANGIFERA SYLVATICA, Roxb. *Chuchi Am, P.*; *Katúr-kúng, L.* E. $\frac{40\text{-}60}{20\text{-}30+6\text{-}8}$ of the M. P. F. *w.* in Terai and L. H. F. valleys up to 3,000 ft. Fl. 4, fr. 7. Is very common in the Dalka Jhar and in the Tista and Great Rangít valleys. Wood good, but very little if ever used; it might do for tea-boxes, and should be tried. The fruit is eaten by the Lepchas.

TAPIRIA HIRSUTA, Hk. f. *Mashul-lara, P.*; *Romchiling-rik, L.* Large climbing shrub of the L. H. F. up to 3,000 ft. Fl. 1, fr. 5.

ODINA WODIER, Roxb. *Bara dabdabbi, P.* L. $\frac{40\text{-}60}{25\text{-}30+5\text{-}8}$ of the S. F., K. S. F. (common), M. P. F. *d.* of Terai and L. H. F. up to 3,000 ft. Fl. 4. Bark dark brown, with small scaly plaits, which fall off. Wood light red, with numerous very narrow medullary rays and large pores, rather regularly distributed; has a very pretty wavy appearance when cut: it works easily and polishes well, but is very heavy. A specimen from Bamunpokri proved to be almost the heaviest wood of the district, weighing as much as 73lb per c. ft.: it had been cut some time, but may not have been sufficiently seasoned. Used by Paharias for cattle-yokes. It gives a brown, clear, brittle gum, used for paper-sizing and in native medicine.

SEMECARPUS ANACARDIUM, Linn. fil. *Bhayla, H.*; *Bhalai, P.*; *Kongki-kúng, L.* E. $\frac{30\text{-}40}{10\text{-}20+3\text{-}4}$ of the S. F., Sv. F., and M. P. F. *w.* of Terai and L. H. F. up to 3,000 ft. Fl. 8, fr. 12. Bark dark brown, exfoliating in roundish scales. Wood dark brown tinged with yellow, with numerous medullary rays, soft. The lower part of the fruit is eaten; the upper part gives a gummy juice, used as marking-ink and sold in the bazars for dhobis' use. It is also used as a vermifuge for sheep and goats by the Paharias.

DRIMYCARPUS RACEMOSUS, Hk. f. *Kagi, P.*; *Brong-kúng, L.* E. $\frac{40\text{-}60}{10\text{-}20+4\text{-}6}$ of the M. H. F. from 3,000 to 6,000 ft. Fl. 3. Wood said to be strong and good. Is very common in the forests of the front face of the Hills, *e.g.* about Tindharia.

SPONDIAS MANGIFERA, Willd. *Ronchiling-kúng, L.* L. $\frac{20\text{-}30}{10\text{-}15+2\text{-}4}$ of the L. H. F. and valleys of the inner hills up to 3,000 ft. Fl. 5, fr. 7.

LEGUMINOSÆ—(1) Papilionaceæ.

PIPTANTHUS NEPALENSIS, D. Don. Large shrub of the Upper Hills from 7,000 to 10,000 ft. Fl. 5, fr. 10. Flowers large, yellow; often seen in gardens in Darjeeling.

CROTALARIA STRIATA, DC. Shrub with yellow flowers; common in waste places in the Terai and Lower Hills. Fl. 8, fr. 12.

CROTALARIA SERICEA, Retz. Shrub, often found in waste places in the Terai and Lower Hills. Fl. 3.

CROTALARIA JUNCEA, Linn. The "sunn" hemp plant; much cultivated in the Terai.

CROTALARIA TETRAGONA, Roxb. *Kengeni, P.*; *Kotulkasub, P.*; *Suhutúng-rúng, L.* Tall shrub, often 6 to 8 ft. high of the Sv. F. in the Terai and L. H. F. on dry slopes. Fl. 10-11, yellow, very handsome; fr. 12-1.

PRIOTROPIS CYTISOIDES, W. and A. *Takpyitmúk, L.* Much branching shrub of the M. Hills, chiefly on old cultivations, from 3,000 to 6,000 ft. Fl. 3, fr. 6. Very common in old cultivations round Kalimpúng and Dumsong.

INDIGOFERA STACHYODES, Ldl. *Chiringi jhar, P.* Large shrub or small tree, often 10-15 ft. high, of the M. H. F. Found in the inner valleys, such as those of the Rangít and Rumaun, up to 5,000 ft. Fl. 7-8, fr. 9-10.

INDIGOFERA PULCHELLA, Roxb. *Hikpi-kúng, L.* Handsome shrub of the undergrowth in the Sâl forests of the Tista and Great Rangít valleys from 2,000 to 3,000 ft. Fl. 1-2. Flowers very pretty, pink.

INDIGOFERA CŒRULEA, Roxb. *Sirisi jhar, P.* Shrub seen once or twice in waste places and by roadsides in the Terai, probably introduced. Fl. 3, fr. 7.

TEPHROSIA CANDIDA, DC. *Bodle-lara, P.*; *Súhútúngrúng, L.* Shrub of the L. and M. H. F. up to 3,000 ft. Common. Fl. 8-9, fr. 12. A very handsome plant, with its white flowers and golden pubescence.

MILLETTIA CINEREA, Bth. *Maukap-rik, L.* Large climber of the L. H. F. up to 4,000 ft. Fl. 2-4.

MILLETTIA MONTICOLA, Kurz. Large handsome climber of the U. H. F. about 6,000 to 7,000 ft. Fl. 5. Common round Darjeeling.

MILLETTIA PACHYCARPA, Bth. *Kojulara, P.*; *Brúdúng, L.* Large climber of the L. H. F. up to 4,000 ft. Fr. 6. Roots give a poison used by the Lepchas for killing fish.

MILLETTIA AURICULATA, Baker. *Brú-rik, L.* Large woody climber of the S. F., K. S. F., M. P. F. *d.* in Terai and L. H. F. up to 3,000 ft. Exceedingly common, especially with Sâl. Fl. 6, fr. 12-1.

SESBANIA ÆGYPTIACA, Pers. *Jait, H.* E. $\frac{15\text{-}20}{0\text{-}5+1\text{-}3}$. Cultivated in the Terai and L. Hills, very fast growing.

DESMODIUM CEPHALOTES, Wall. *Bodle-kúrú, P.*; *Maniph-tyol, L.* Shrub, 4 to 5 ft. high, of the Terai S. F. and L. H. F. up to 2,000 ft. Fl. 7, fr. 1. Recognized by its triquetrous stems. with dense silvery, silky pubescence.

DESMODIUM PULCHELLUM, Bth. Shrub, common in S. F., Sv. F. and M. P. F. *d.* in Terai and L. H. F. up to 2,000 ft. Fl. 5-6, fr. 7-11. Recognized by its flowers being enclosed in 2-foliolate bracts in a long spiciform raceme.

DESMODIUM FLORIBUNDUM, G. Don. Large shrub, common in the L. and M. H. F. up to 4,000 ft., especially in old cultivation in rather dry places. Fl. 10, fr. 12. Recognized by its densely crowded racemes of large blue flowers, big bracts, and silky many-jointed pods.

DESMODIUM CONFERTUM, DC. *Chiptikurú, P.* Large straggling shrub of the undergrowth in the Sâl forests of the Tista and Great Rangít rivers. Fl. 11, fr. 1. Has smaller racemes of flowers and fewer jointed pods than *D. floribundum.*

DESMODIUM LATIFOLIUM, DC. *Chepekúrú. P.* Erect undershrub of the S. F. and M. P. F. *d.* in the Terai and L. H. F. to 3,000 ft., especially in Sâl forests. Fl. 5, fr. 10. Recognized by its unifoliolate, round, cordate leaflets, and erect, unbranching growth.

DESMODIUM POLYCARPUM, DC. *Bolú, P.*; *Tirhyúkmyok, L.* Branching shrub, often quite small, of the L. and M. H. F. up to 5,000 ft. Very common. Fl. 8-9. Recognized by its angular, densely hairy stem and small round leaflets.

DESMODIUM GYRANS, DC. *Bolú, P.* Erect-growing shrubby plant, often 4-5 ft. high, of the S. F., Sv. F. and M. P. F.

in Terai and L. H. F. up to 3,000 ft. Fl. 7-8, fr. 10-2. Recognized by its two small lateral sensitive leaflets. Very common at Bamunpokri.

DESMODIUM GYROIDES, DC. *Bolú, P.* Shrub $\frac{10\text{-}15}{0\text{-}3+1\text{-}1}$ of the Sv. F., S. F. and M. P. F. *d.* in the Terai, also in L. H. F. up to 3,000 ft. Fl. fr. 9-2. Very common all over the Terai. Recognized by its tall woody growth and bright purple flowers. Side leaflets generally suppressed.

ABRUS PRECATORIUS, Linn.; ABRUS PULCHELLUS, Wall. *Maspati-lara, P.* Slender climbers of the Terai and L. H. F. up to 3,000 ft. Fl. fr. 10-1.

ERYTHRINA (STRICTA, Roxb.). *Fullidha, P.*; *Katiang-kúng, L.* L. $\frac{40\text{-}60}{20\text{-}40+4\text{-}6}$ of the K. S. F. in the Terai and banks of rivers in the L. H. F. valleys. Also common in low waste ground near rivers in the Terai. Fl. 1, fr. 11. Wood very soft, spongy. Bark prickly, smooth, grey-green, thickly corky when older. (I think there are two species, and they are probably *E. stricta* and *E. suberosa*, but specimens are difficult to get and very difficult to preserve when procured.)

ERYTHRINA ARBORESCENS, Roxb. *Fullidha, P.*; *Rodinga, P.*; *Gyesa-kúng, L.* L. $\frac{20\text{-}30}{10\text{-}15+3\text{-}4}$ of the M. and U. H. F. from 5,000 to 7,000 ft. Very commonly planted in Darjeeling. Fl. fr. 1-2. Wood soft, light, useless. It is very handsome when covered with its bright scarlet flowers, but it is rather unsightly when bare of leaves. Any branch or twig will strike root, and felled logs send out branches, which root at once.

SPATHOLOBUS ROXBURGHII, Bth. *Debre-lara, P.*; *Terol-rik, L.* A huge climber of the S. F. and M. P. F. *d.* in Terai and L. H. F. up to 3,000 ft. Fl. 8, fr. 1. It often reaches 3-4 ft. in girth. Wood soft, in concentric layers separated by a ring of soft tissue, exuding a copious red astringent gum resembling "kino." Flowers white; fruit red, with usually a drop of gum exuding on either side of the single seed; leaves trifoliolate.

BUTEA FRONDOSA, Roxb. *Palass, H.*; *Palasi, P.*; *Laho-kúng, L.* L. $\frac{30\text{-}40}{10\text{-}20+4\text{-}6}$ of the Sv. F. in the Terai. Fl. 3, fr. 5-6. Bark grey-brown, soft, spongy. Wood dirty white colour, quite useless. It gives a clear gum, which is rarely used. When in flower it is very handsome, being then a mass of scarlet and black: but otherwise it is a very ugly tree, with a crooked twisted stem and ungainly branches. It is rarely found except in long grass Savannahs, such as Tirihana and Khadma, to the north of the Dalka Jhar. A dye is sometimes extracted from the flowers.

BUTEA (MINOR, Ham.). *Bolatru, P.*; *Namosinglet-kúng, L.* Large shrub or climber of the L. H. F. on dry slopes, and only west of the Balasan, towards the Nepal frontier. Leaves very large, silky—tomentose. Fr. 1.

MUCUNA IMBRICATA, DC. *Balengra, P.*; *Kouatch, P.*; *Dangnyim-rik, L.* Climber of the banks of streams, waste places, and M. P. F. *d.* in the Terai. Fl. 11, fr. 1. Fruit covered with plaits on both sides, and armed with stinging hairs.

MUCUNA SP. *Balengra, P.*; *Taknyeérik, L.* A huge climber of the M. P. F. *w.* of Terai (very common in Dalka Jhar) and L. H. F. valleys. Fl. 1-2, fr. 6-7. Fruit long, flat, velvety, covered with dense short stinging hairs.

MUCUNA MACROCARPA, Wall. *Balengra, P.*; *Taknyeérik, L.* An enormous climber of the M. and U. H. F. from 4,000 to 7,000 ft. Fl. 5, fr. 8. The biggest climber of the hills, and exceedingly common. A very large one of 3 to 4 ft. girth may be seen at Darjeeling by the side of the road leading from the Club to the bazaar, and it is very common at Puttabong and Lebong. Flowers dirty yellow-white. Fruit very long, rather twisted, and swollen round the seeds. Leaves trifoliolate. Wood very soft, spongy.

MUCUNA PRURIENS, DC. *Kouatch, P.*; *Kajúkop-rik, L.* Is an annual, but it is so very common in the Terai and L. H. F., and is found climbing to such a height over big trees, that it is as well to mention it. Fl. 6-7, fr. 1, covered with golden brown very stinging hairs, which cause great irritation. I have never seen it anywhere so common as on the northern boundary of Chenga forest.

PUERARIA TUBEROSA, DC. *Debre-lara, P.*; *Lungom-rik, L.* L. large climber of the K. S. F. and M. P. F. *d.* in Terai and L. H. F. up to 3,000 ft. Fl. 2-3, blue, in handsome racemes, when the shrub is leafless. Wood soft, spongy.

PUERARIA WALLICHII, DC. *Debre-lara, P.* Climbing shrub of the L. H. F. west of the Balasan, up to 2,000 ft., chiefly with Sâl. Fl. 10-11, fr. 1-2.

FLEMINGIA STRICTA, Roxb. *Batwasi, P.* Shrub of the undergrowth in S. F. and M. P. F. *d.* in Terai and L. Hills. Fl. 2. Grows to 6-10 ft. high. Easily recognized by its triquetrous stems and dense racemes with long bracts.

FLEMINGIA STROBILIFERA, R. Br. *Bolú, P.* Shrub, common in the undergrowth of the S. F. and M. P. F. *d.* and on waste places in Terai. Recognized by its flowers, enclosed in large semicircular folded bracts.

FLEMINGIA SEMIALATA, Roxb. *Batwasi, P.*; *Mipitmúk, L.* Large tall shrub of the Terai and L. H. F. up to 4,000 ft. Chiefly common on the hills and in Sâl forest. Fl. 9, fr. 12. Flowers pink, in dense racemes. Fruit small, round, with two black seeds.

FLEMINGIA INVOLUCRATA, Bth. A large shrub of the lower Terai, chiefly in the meadows between the Sâl jhars. Fl. 11, in dense soft heads, blue.

DALBERGIA SISSOO, Roxb. *Sissú, H. P.* L. $\frac{40\text{-}60}{15\text{-}30+4\text{-}6}$ of the K. S. F. in Terai. Fl. 3, fr. 8-11. Bark light brown, exfoliating longitudinally in narrow strips. Wood brown, close-grained, hard, very good; it is chiefly used for making carts, for furniture, doors and windows, and occasionally for beams and planking. The forests of sissú are scattered along most of the Terai rivers: it is found gregariously on the Tista; partly so, but mixed with khair, in the proportion of 1 to 3, on the Mahanadi; and on the Balasan and Mechi rivers in mixture with a large variety of other trees. The only big timber now available is in the forests of the latter rivers. It is being planted at Bamunpokri, and seems to thrive there, although naturally it is only found on the gravelly lands of the broad beds of the rivers. Seedlings come up self-sown in great abundance, but when once up require a great deal of light. The seeds remain long on the tree. The weight of a few specimens from the Terai (Rakti forest chiefly) gave an average of 45℔ per c. ft.

DALBERGIA LATIFOLIA, Roxb. *Sitsal*; *Sitisal, P.* L. $\frac{20\text{-}30}{5\text{-}10+2\text{-}3}$ of the Sv. F. and M. P. F. *d.* in Terai and L. H. F. up to 2,000 ft. Chiefly common to the west of the Mahanadi. Fl. 8, fr. 1. Bark grey, peeling off in small flakes. Wood: sapwood white, sometimes very little only, especially in hill specimens,; sometimes broad, chiefly in plains specimens: heartwood when first cut dark purple-brown with occasional darker layers, afterwards turning black-brown, hard, heavy. The average of specimens from Bamunpokri gave 50℔ per c. ft. Very valuable for furniture and door and window frames. Largely used for "kukri" handles and small articles, such as boxes. It is now only found as a small tree; but, judging from the size of old stumps occasionally seen in the forest, it was formerly found of much larger size, but has been cut out. This, too, seems confirmed by the statements of Nepalese, who assert that only a very short distance on their side of the frontier it is to be found of very large size. Easily propagated by seed.

DALBERGIA FOLIACEA, Wall. *Tatebiri, P.* Large straggling shrub of the M. P. F. *w.* in Terai; chiefly in the lower parts, *e.g.* the south of the Dalka Jhar. Fl. 4, fr. 1.

DALBERGIA TAMARINDIFOLIA, Roxb. *Damar, P.*; *Teihyaprik, L.*; *Shengrik, L.* Large climbing shrub of the M. P. F. *w.* and banks of streams in the Terai and L. H. F. valleys to 2,000 ft. Fl. 3, fr. 4-5.

DALBERGIA (LANCEOLARIA, Linn.). *Bander Siris, P.* L. large tree of the K. S. F. and banks of rivers in Terai. Fl. 3. Wood yellowish white, rather heavy. It much resembles a *siris* in appearance.

DALBERGIA STIPULACEA, Roxb. *Tatebiri, P.*; *Garodosal, M.*; *Tón-nyok, L.* Large climbing tree of the S. F., K. S. F. and M. P. F. *d.* in Terai and L. H. F. up to 3,000 ft. Fl. 8, fr. 12-2. Bark dark brown, rough. Wood pink-grey, hard, close-grained, very prettily marked with lines of different colours. The c. ft. weighs 45℔.

DALBERGIA STENOCARPA, Kurz. *Bander Siris, P.*; *Tatebiri, P.*; *Balphet-kúng, L.* L. $\frac{40\text{-}60}{20\text{-}30+4\text{-}6}$ of the L. H. F. up to 3,000 ft. and occasionally in K. S. F. in Terai, as at Sivoke. It is commonest towards the Nepal frontier. A handsome tree. Fl. 5, fr. 7. Wood rather soft. This is perhaps the same as *D. hircina*, Bth.

DERRIS CUNEIFOLIA, Bth. L. $\frac{30\text{-}40}{15\text{-}20+3\text{-}4}$. A common tree of the L. H. F. up to 3,000 ft. Fl. 4, fr. 6-7. Very pretty when in flower and young leaf, as it has then golden-brown leaves and long racemes of lilac-coloured flowers.

PONGAMIA GLABRA, Vent. *Sadun, P.* Large tree of the L. H. F. I have only seen it in the forests west of the Balasan, viz. Chenga and Lohagarhi. Wood said to be strong and good.

(2) Cæsalpinieæ.

MEZONEURUM CUCULLATUM, W. & A. *Sungray, P.*; *Rung-gong, L.*; *Yangkup, L.* Large straggling climber of the M. P. F. in Terai and L. and M. H. F. up to 5,000 ft. Stems covered with corky tubercles, each bearing strong-hooked prickles. Fl. 9, fr. 1. Flowers yellow.

CÆSALPINIA BONDUCELLA, Roxb. *Yangkup, L.* Large straggling shrub of the banks of streams in the Terai, chiefly in the lower part, *e.g.* about Phansidewa, where it forms dense bushes. Fl. fr. 1-3, flowers yellow. Fruit covered with prickles, and bearing hard-shelled grey seeds.

ACROCARPUS FRAXINIFOLIUS, Arnott. *Mandania, P.*; *Madling-kúng, L.* L. $\frac{100\text{-}120}{60\text{-}80+8\text{-}12}$ of the L. H. F. up to 4,000 ft. Chiefly in valleys. Commoner in the Dumsong than in the western forests. Fine trees in the Rungdung and Balasan valleys and round Dalingkot. Fl. 3, fr. 12-2. Wood dark red, hard, strong, easily worked, is now coming into use for tea-boxes, planking, and all purposes. It promises to become very valuable, and, as it is very fast growing, should not be neglected in replanting banks of streams and forests in the Lower Hills, where Sâl will not grow. A most beautiful, stately tree, with lofty cylindrical stem and branches, beginning only at a great height. Leaves large bi-pinnate. Flowers orange, in handsome spikes.

CASSIA FISTULA, Linn. *Amultas, H.*; *Raj Birij, P.* L. $\frac{60\text{-}80}{40\text{-}50+4\text{-}6}$ of the M. P. F. *d.* in the Terai and L. H. F. up to 2,000 ft. Fl. 8, fr. 12. Bark brown, peeling off in small rectangular scales, leaving the inner white bark exposed. Wood light red, turning darker with exposure, very hard, heavy (workmen object to using it, as it blunts their tools), has a beautiful grain and planes very well. Annual rings very distinct. Specimens from Bamunpokri gave 64lb per c. ft. It is much esteemed by the Nepalese. It is often planted for ornament, having long pendulous racemes of yellow fragrant flowers. The fruit is a long cylindrical indehiscent pod, the pulp of which is much used as a purgative. Should be grown in regenerating dry mixed forests in the Terai, where Sâl will not grow.

CASSIA OBOVATA, Coll. *Tapyitnyok, L.* A diffuse herbaceous plant from a perennial root-stock; found in all waste places in Terai, and as under-growth in K. S. F. in company with the annual *C. occidentalis*. Fl. 7, fr. 11-12.

BAUHINIA MALABARICA, Roxb. *Karmai, Bg.*; *Taki, P.* E. $\frac{30\text{-}40}{10\text{-}20+4\text{-}5}$ of the S. F., Sv. F., M. P. F. *d.* in Terai and L. H. F. up to 2,000 ft. Fl. 9, fr. 1-2. A small tree with a spreading crown. Wood reddish brown, hard, heavy, not used. The leaves are acid and are eaten, as are also the seeds.

BAUHINIA PURPUREA, Linn. *Amil taki, P.*; *Kachik-kúng, L.* E. $\frac{30\text{-}50}{10\text{-}20+4\text{-}6}$ of the M. P. F. *d.* in Terai and L. H. F. up to 4,000 ft. Common in the inner valleys. Fl. 10-11, fr. 2-3. A handsome tree with two varieties—one with red, the other with white flowers. Wood said to be rather soft, not used. Seeds eaten by Lepchas.

BAUHINIA VARIEGATA, L. *Kachnar, H.*; *Khwairalo, P.*; *Rha-kúng, L.* L. $\frac{20\text{-}30}{10\text{-}15 + 2\text{-}3.}$ of the Sv. F. and M. P. F. *d.* in Terai, but chiefly in L. H. F. up to 2,000 ft. on dry exposures. Fl. 3-4. Wood greyish brown, rather close-grained, easily worked. Is a most beautiful tree when in full flower, having large white azalea-like flowers with usually one red petal. They are eaten by the Paharias. It is leafless when in flower, and is all the more handsome, as this occurs at a season when the country is very much dried up.

BAUHINIA VAHLII, W. and A. *Borla, P.*; *Sungung-rik, L.* A gigantic climber of the S. F., M. P. F. *d.* in Terai and L. H. F. up to 3,000 ft. Fl. 4, fr. 1-2. The stems often reach 4 ft. or more in girth. Wood very curious, consisting of a quadrangular cross-shaped centre, surrounded by irregular masses of porous wood separated by spongy tissue. The bark of the long climbing shoots is used to make rough ropes. It gives a copious gum, of no use. The fruit is large, broad, softly pubescent, bursting with a loud report to let loose the flat seeds, which are roasted and eaten. The flowers are cream white, very pretty, and the leaves often 12-18 in. long by as much broad. They are used for plates and in the construction of "ghooms," the mat umbrellas used by Paharia coolies in the rainy season. It is the chief big creeper of the Sâl forests.

BAUHINIA ANGUINA, Roxb. *Naiwilli-lara, P.*; *Suhutúngrúng-rik, L.* A large climber of the M. P. F. *w.* in Terai and L. H. F. valleys up to 2,000 ft. Its stem has a very curious growth: when young it is twisted alternately one way and the other; as it gets older, it becomes more cylindrical, with a raised ridge round it in the form of the thread of a screw. The bark is used to make ropes, which are very strong.

BAUHINIA (MACROPHYLLA). *Kala khwairahlo, P.* A large climber of the L. H. F. about 1,000 to 2,000 ft. Not common.

TAMARINDUS INDICA, Linn. *Imli, H.*; *Titri, P.* The tamarind tree. Cultivated in villages in the Terai, but sparingly, for its fruit.

(3) Mimoseæ.

ENTADA SCANDENS, Bth. *Pangra, P.*; *Taktokhyem, L.* A very big climber of the M. P. F. *d.* in Terai and L. H. F. up to 2,000 ft. Fl. 3, fr. 12. Bark rough. Stem much twisted, like the strands of an enormous cable. Wood very soft, porous. The fruit is often two or more feet long, with very big seeds. The Lepchas eat these after long soaking and roasting to extract the poison. They are used by the Paharias in washing the hair.

MIMOSA RUBICAULIS, Lamk. *Aradi, P.*; *Sibriu-kúng, L.* E. (?) $\frac{10\text{-}20.}{0\text{-}3 + \frac{1}{2}\text{-}1\frac{1}{2}.}$ of the Sv. F. and undergrowth in S. F. and M. P. F. *d.* in the Terai and L. H. F. up to 3,000 ft. Fl. 8-9, fr. 1-2. Bark brown, thin, with scattered prickles. Wood light red, with bands of white or yellowish white, hard, close-grained.

MIMOSA PUDICA, Willd. *Lajima, P.* Small shrub of the Terai, often growing under favourable circumstances to 6 ft. in height. Probably introduced, as it is only found within a short distance of frequented roads.

ACACIA CATECHU, Willd. *Khair.* L. $\frac{20\text{-}40}{10\text{-}15 + 3\text{-}4}$ of the K. S. F. in Terai. Fl. 7, fr. 1. Bark dark brown, exfoliating in long narrow strips. Wood red, hard, easily worked, durable. (Specimens examined gave 48-50℔ per c. ft., but the wood of old trees is often heavier.) Used for cotton rollers and other purposes by the Nepalese. Is being tried for sleepers, and will probably do well. Makes splendid charcoal, and is one of the best of fire-woods. The Nepalese say the lac insect is found on it. Cutch is rarely extracted here, and does not seem to be so in Nepal; but I have heard of it being occasionally done by the Bhutanese. The stem is often deeply indented, so that even if the tree grew straight it would be difficult to get big scantlings out of it. It will give 6 ft. sleepers though, and without much waste, as there is very little sapwood. The tree grows very gregariously on the Mahanadi and Tista rivers, but on the Balasan and Mechi it is generally mixed with numerous other kinds of trees. The chief forest is that on the Mahanadi.

ACACIA (FERRUGINEA, DC.). *Khour, P.*; *Kankar, P.* L. $\frac{50\text{-}60}{20\text{-}30 + 4\text{-}6}$ of the S. F., Sv. F. and M. P. F. *d.* in Terai. Bark dark coloured, peeling of in small square scales, leaving the white inner bark very conspicuous. Wood yellowish brown when young, turning dark red-brown when old. Probably the hardest wood in the district; heavy (specimens gave young trees 52℔, old thoroughly seasoned wood 70℔ per c. ft.). Medullary rays very numerous, fine, with large pores and very indistinct annual rings. Old logs of large size are often found in the forest; they give a very fine description of charcoal, but the wood is difficult to cut, as it turns the edges of country axes and spoils a saw. Old "kala-khambas" of trees are found in great quantity on land which has been cleared by Mechis, *e.g.* at Mohurgong.

NOTE.—There may possibly be two species, *Khour* and *Kankar*. I have put the name *ferruginea* doubtfully, as the descriptions of that tree seem to come nearest; but the leaflets are much larger, and indeed about four to five times larger and many times fewer than those of *A. ferruginea* in Colonel Beddome's figure. In appearance it resembles *Albizzia odoratissima*.

ACACIA CÆSIA, W. and A. *Harari, P.*; *Payir-rik, L.*; *Ngræm-rik, L.* A large prickly climber of the M. P. F. *d.* in Terai and L. H. F. up to 3,000 ft. Fl. 8, fr. 3. Bark smooth, grey, used by Lepchas for washing the hair. Stem deeply cleft many times, the ridges twisting upwards like a screw. Wood light yellow, inner hard, outer soft, with numerous fine medullary rays and large pores.

ACACIA CONCINNA, DC. *Toldúng, L.* Large, very prickly climbing shrub of the M. P. F. *d.* and K. S. F. and by banks of streams in Lower Terai. Fl. 3, fr. 1-3. The fruit is thick and fleshy, it is used for washing the hair.

ACACIA PENNATA, Willd. *Tol-rik, L.* A very large climbing shrub of the S. F. and M. P. F. *d.* in Terai and L. H. F. up to 3,000 feet; climbing over the tallest trees. Very prickly. Fl. 4, fr. 12. Bark reddish brown. Wood reddish, very soft and porous, with large vessels and numerous medullary rays.

ALBIZZIA LUCIDA, Bth. *Ngraem-kúng, L.* L. $\frac{40\text{-}50}{15\text{-}20+3\text{-}5}$ of the L. H. F., especially valleys, where it is generally found by the banks of rivers, up to 2,000 ft. Fl. 3, fr. 1-2, easily recognized from other *Albizzias* by its very few large leaflets, and from *Pithecolobium* by its straight pod.

ALBIZZIA ODORATISSIMA, Bth. *Siris, P.*; *Tedong-kúng, L.* L. $\frac{40\text{-}80}{30\text{-}40+4\text{-}6}$ of the L. H. F. Not very common. Fl. 5, fr. 1-2. Bark grey-brown, wrinkled. Wood dark reddish brown, strong, hard, heavy (the average of several Bamunpokri specimens gave 55lb per c. ft.), is easily worked. A fine timber. Recognized by its tall straight trunk, and small, rather pendulous, branches.

ALBIZZIA PROCERA, Bth. *Safed siris, P.*; *Takmur-kúng, L.* L. $\frac{40\text{-}60}{20\text{-}30+6\text{-}8}$ of the K. S. F. and M. P. F. *d.* in Terai and L. H. F., especially on level spots on the banks of rivers. Fl. 8-9, fr. 1-2. Bark light brown, peeling off in small scales, leaving the yellow inner bark very conspicuous. Wood almost exactly like that of *A. odoratissima*, but much lighter. (Average Terai specimens 36lb per c. ft.) Occasionally used, I believe, for tea-boxes and in building, and much esteemed by planters for charcoal. It is easily recognized by its tall white stem and big spreading branches. Gives a clear gum, not used.

ALBIZZIA (LEBBEK, Bth.). *Sedong-kúng, L.* Tree of the L. H. F. Not common. Has rather large leaflets with reticulated veins. Fl. 7, fr. 11-12.

ALBIZZIA (JULIBRISSIN, Boivin). *Sedong-kúng, L.* Tree of the M. P. F. *d.* in Terai and L. H. F. Not very common. Has ashy-green foliage, small leaflets, and tomentose racemes. Fl. 4.

ALBIZZIA STIPULATA, Boivin. *Kala siris, P.*; *Singriang-kúng, L.* L. $\frac{40\text{-}60}{30\text{-}40+6\text{-}10}$ of the K. S. F. and M. P. F. *d.* in Terai and L. and M. H F. up to 5,000 ft. Fl. 4-6, fr. 2-3. Bark greyish black, with deep horizontal folds; outer bark exfoliating in small scales. Wood resembling that of *A. odoratissima* and *A. procera*, but very much lighter (Terai specimens gave 28-30℔ per c. ft.) Has been used for tea-boxes, I believe, and for this it would probably do well. It is used by Lepchas for the sheath of their "ban," or long straight knife. Sapwood rather large, decays very rapidly. Easily recognized by its dark thick trunk, horizontal wide-spreading branches, and flat-topped crown. Leaflets very numerous, with big stipules. It gives a very copious gum, used for paper size, which will probably be found to be about the best of the gums in the district.

PITHECOLOBIUM ANGULATUM, Bth. *Takpyitnyok, L.* Large tree of the M. P. F. *w.* in Terai and L. H. F. valleys. Very handsome. Fl. 4.

PITHECOLOBIUM BIGEMINUM, Mart. *Takpyit-kúng, L.* L. $\frac{15\text{-}20}{10\text{-}15+2\text{-}3}$ of the L. and M. H. F. up to 4,000 ft. Fl. 3, fr. 7. Seeds eaten by Lepchas.

NOTE.—Many ornamental trees and shrubs of this family are also found in gardens, such are the broom, *Sarothamnus vulgaris*, Wimmer; the furze, *Ulex Europæus*, L.; and the laburnum, *Cytisus Laburnum*, L. A few fine plants of *Gastanospermum Australe* may be seen at Bamunpokri, planted, I believe, in 1869 by Mr. Leeds.

ROSACEÆ.

PRUNUS PERSICA, Bth. and Hook. f. *Aru, P.*; *Takpo-kúng, L.* The peach. Very commonly cultivated in Darjeeling, but does not ripen its fruit sufficiently for eating unless cooked. In the Terai it is capable of being cultivated to a great degree of perfection. Fl. 3, fr. 8-9.

PRUNUS PUDDUM, Roxb. *Paddam, P.*; *Kongki-kúng, L.* L. $\frac{60\text{-}80}{30\text{-}40+8\text{-}12}$ of the M. and U. H. F. up to 6,000 ft. Common as a small tree in second-growth forest and in some forests at about 6,000 ft., such as Sepoydura, Tukdah, and round Dumsong. Bark grey, smooth, papery when young; when older, rough, hard, reddish brown, peeling off horizontally. Wood red or reddish brown, scented, hard, close-grained, with numerous medullary rays and well-defined annual rings. Weighs about 40-45℔ per c. ft. Used to make furniture, for which it is very good. There are two varieties:—

No. 1.—Very big tree; crimson flowers, appearing in March.

No. 2.—Smaller tree; pink or white flowers, October–November.

PRUNUS PADUS, Linn. *Likh-aru, P.*; *Hhosahlot-kúng, L.* L. $\frac{40\text{-}60}{20\text{-}30+6\text{-}8}$ of the M. and U. H. F. from 6,000 to 10,000 ft. Fl. 5, fr. 10-11. Fruits eaten by hillmen. Bark black-grey, smooth, thin. Wood—sapwood large, white; heartwood red-brown, with numerous medullary rays and pretty grain, polishes well. It is very common about Darjeeling, and is one of the first trees to come into new leaf in March. It grows very quickly, with curious verticillate upright growing branches.

PRUNUS FERRUGINEA, Wall. L. $\frac{20\text{-}30}{10\text{-}15+4\text{-}5}$ of the R. F. and F. F. especially about 11,000 ft. Fl. ?, fr. 10.

PRUNUS ACUMINATUS, Roxb. Small tree of the M. and U. H. F. to 6,000 ft. Fl. 3, fr. ? Not common.

PRUNUS SP. *Kamki, Bh.* L. $\frac{20\text{-}30}{10\text{-}15+3\text{-}4}$ of the R. F., from 9,000 ft. to 11,000 ft. Found on Tongloo. Wood red, hard, and close-grained, sweet-scented.

NOTE.—The plum (*P. communis*, Huds.), cherry (*P. cerasus*, L.), and apricot (*P. Armeniaca*, L.), have all been, and are still, occasionally cultivated by residents in Darjeeling and planters. The almond I have never heard of.

PYGEUM ACUMINATUM, Colebr. Tree of the M. P. F. *w.* I have only once seen it on the Panchenai river near Sukna depôt.

SPIRÆA CALLOSA, Lal. *Shimbengnyok, L.* Shrub of U. H. F. 7,000 to 8,000 ft., especially in cleared places, *e.g.* Darjeeling station. Fl. 7, fr. 1-2.

NOTE.—Two or three ornamental species of *Spiræa* are cultivated in Darjeeling.

NEILLIA THYRSIFLORA, Don. *Pukshioung-rik, L.* Shrub of cleared places in U. Hills, *e.g.* Darjeeling station, where very common. Fl. 8-12, fr. 1-2.

RUBUS MOLUCCANUS. *Bipemkanta, P.*; *Sufok-ji, L.* A straggling shrub, of various forms, and found from the plains up to 10,000 ft. Is probably the same as *R. rugosus*, Gm. Easily known by its 3 to 5-lobed wrinkled leaves. Fruit edible, but mawkish. Fl. 7-8, fr. 9-10.

RUBUS THOMSONI, Focke. Shrub, diffuse, from 7,000 to 10,000 ft. Leaves trifoliolate, green. Fl. 9-10, fr. 11-12.

RUBUS NIVEUS, Wall. Shrub of F. F. or, more properly, of the grass slopes from 10,000 to 12,000 ft. Fl. 10.

RUBUS MACROCARPUS, King. *Fatsiphok, L.* Straggling shrub of U. H. F. Common in Rungbool plantation. Has an enormous fruit, often 1 in. to 1½ in. diameter. Easily recognized by this and by the large flowers and long-tailed sepals. Fl. 5, fr. 8-9. Fruit eaten by Lepchas.

RUBUS FLAVUS, Ham. *Tolu Aselu, P.*; *Kashyem, L.* A large straggling shrub with yellow edible fruits of very good flavour; in fact, the two species of *Actinidia* and one or two other *Rubi* are, with this, the only properly edible wild fruits in the district. Common from 3,000 to 7,000 ft., especially in old 'joomed' land. Has a general resemblance to the blackberry. Wood rather hard, with big medullary rays and reddish brown prickly bark. Fl. 3, fr. 4-5. There is a var. *incisus* with deeply dentate leaves.

Rubus calycinus, Wall. A small trailing shrub, with red edible berries, found round Darjeeling. Fl. 4-5, fr. 7-8. The "ground raspberry."

Rubus pulcherrimus, Hk. *Kalé Aselu, P.*; *Hlotumbrik, L.* A straggling thornless shrub, with very handsome trifoliolate leaves, silvery beneath. Common about 7,000 ft., especially round Darjeeling, and thence up to Tongloo, 10,000 ft. Fl. 8-9, fr. 10-11.

Rubus lineatus, Rwdt. *Gempé Aselu, P.* A large shrub without thorns and with 5-foliolate leaves, silvery beneath, like the preceding. 'It has a red edible fruit. It covers the hillside everywhere about 6,000 to 8,000 ft., where the forest has been cleared, *e.g.* the Rungbool plantation. Stems up to 2 or 3 in. diameter, of a pink colour, and with bark peeling off in flakes. Fl. 8-9, fr. 10-11.

Rubus paniculatus, Sm. *Numing-rik, L.* Straggling shrub, common from 6,000 to 8,000 ft. Recognized by its simple cordate leaves with yellow tomentum beneath. Fl. 7.

Rubus acuminatus, Sm. *Sané Aselu*; *Numing-rik, L.*; *Siritakdangji, L.* Resembles the preceding, except that the leaves are glabrous and green on both sides. Fl. 7.

Rubus Sikkimensis, O. Kze. *Pohong, L.* A large straggling thorny shrub, with a big red edible, though rather insipid, fruit. Fl. 4, fr. 6-7.

Rubus macilentus, Camb. Resembles the preceding, but is much smaller and has yellow fruit. Fl. ?, fr. 5-6.

Rubus asper, Don. A large straggling thorny shrub, 6,000 to 8,000 ft.

Rubus lasiocarpus, Sm. *Kajutalam, L.* A large straggling thorny shrub, very common round Darjeeling. Fruit small, black-glaucous, hairy, and of good flavour. Fl. 4-5, fr. 7-8.

Note.—Both the raspberry and blackberry are occasionally cultivated in Darjeeling.

Potentilla frutescens, Linn. Small stiff-branched shrub, common on rocks on the Singalila range at 11,000 to 12,000 ft., in company with *Rhododendron lepidotus*. It has handsome yellow flowers and silvery foliage.

Rosa sericea, Ldl. Small tree or large shrub of R. F. and F. F. above 10,000 ft. Fl. 6, fr. 10. Wood hard, close-grained, with prominent medullary rays, very pretty. Grows to ¾ to 1 ft. in girth.

Pyrus communis, Linn. The pear is cultivated in the Darjeeling district. It thrives best at about 5,000 ft. elevation, but the fruit is always hard, though good for baking. Fl. 3-4, fr. 9-10. The "apple" I have never seen.

Pyrus variolosa, Wall. *Likúng.* L. $\frac{10\text{-}20}{5\text{-}10+2\text{-}3}$. I have only seen one specimen not far from the Tasingthong Monastery at 5,000 ft., and that probably planted. Fl. 3.

Pyrus cuspidata, Linn. $\frac{40\text{-}60}{20\text{-}30+4\text{-}6}$. Big tree of R. F. above 9,000 ft. Large specimens may be seen on the Surmonbong spur below Tongloo. Fl. ?, fr. 11.

Pyrus foliolosa, Wall. Sometimes a tree, sometimes, and more often, growing on other trees, like *Ficus* or *Wightia*, 7,000 to 10,000 ft. Foliage resembles that of *P. aucuparia, Gærtn.* Fl. 5, fr. 7-10.

Pyrus microphylla, Wall. L. $\frac{20\text{-}30}{5\text{-}10+2\text{-}3}$ from 9,000 to 12,000 ft. Much resembles the preceding, but has much smaller leaflets. It may be a variety. Fl. ?, fr. 9-10.

Pyrus lanata, Don. *Singka, Bh.* L. $\frac{40\text{-}50}{20\text{-}30+4\text{-}6}$. Large tree of R. F. from 8,000 to 10,000 ft. Very easily remarked, even at a distance, by the shining whiteness of the under surface of the leaves. Fl. ?, fr. 10. Fruit edible, about ½ in. diameter.

Pyrus sp. *Tungru-kúng, L.* L. big tree of U. H. F. from 6.000 to 8,000 ft., resembling the last, but the under surface of the leaves has a very woolly tomentum. Fl. ?, fr. 9.

Pyrus sp. *Kumbool-kúng, L.* L. tree, or more often epiphytic tree, from seeds left in the branches of other trees by birds, as in *P. foliolosa.* Differs from the last three by its almost entirely glabrous leaves. Found in U. H. F. about 7,000 to 8,000 ft. Fl. 5, fr. 7-8.

Pyrus Indica, Roxb. *Li-kúng, L.* L. $\frac{30\text{-}40}{10\text{-}15+4\text{-}6}$ of the M. H. F. from 3,000 to 5,000 ft. Found by me at Munggor, near Kalimpúng. Leaves of young plants much divided and almost glabrous, resembling those of *Cratægus Oxyacantha.* Those of big trees covered, as well as the stipules, young shoots, and calyx, with dense white tomentum. Fl. 3, fr. ? Fruit edible.

Pyrus. L. $\frac{30\text{-}40}{10\text{-}20+1\text{-}3}$ of the M. P. F. *w.* in Terai. Found by me in the Dalka Jhar forest, where it is common. Fl. 2-3, fr. ?

Cratœgus Oxyacantha, Linn. The Hawthorn. A few good specimens may be seen in gardens in Darjeeling.

Cotoneaster microphylla, Wall. Small prostrate shrub of F. F. about 11,000 ft. Found on the rocks about Sundukpho. Fl. ?, fr. 9-10.

Photinia dubia, Ldl. *Berkúng, L.* E. $\frac{10\text{-}30}{0\text{-}10+1\text{-}3}$ of the U. H. F. from 5,000 to 7,000 ft. Very common in forests round Dumsong. Fl. 10-11. Recognized by its shining, deeply crenate leaves.

Photinia integrifolia, Ldl. *Shumbul-kúng, L.* E. $\frac{10\text{-}20}{0\text{-}5+1\text{-}3}$ U. H. F. from 5,000 to 7,000 ft. Common about Darjeeling and Dumsong. Fl. 5, fr. 11. Recognized by its smooth undivided leaves.

Photinia sp. *Yelnyo, L.* E. $\frac{20\text{-}40}{10\text{-}20+2\text{-}4}$ of the U. H. F. Common about Darjeeling. Fl. 5, fr 9-10. Recognized by its large leaves, serrate above, undivided below, and ferruginously tomentose beneath and on the shoots and petioles. Bark yellowish, wrinkled, thin. Wood pink-white, with rather dark, medullary rays and scattered medullary spots, hard, close-grained; does not warp.

Eriobotrya macrocarpa, Kz. Small tree of the L. H. F. up to 3,000 ft. valleys. Fl. ?, fr. 11.

SAXIFRAGACEÆ.

Hydrangea robusta, Hk. f. and T. *Bogoti, P.* L. $\frac{20\text{-}30}{10\text{-}15+2\text{-}3}$ of the U. H. F. Very common about Darjeeling and in the Rungbool and Rungyrúm forests as an undergrowth. Very handsome when in flower with its bright blue fertile and large cream-coloured sterile flowers. Fl. 9, fr. 12-1. Wood white, with many fine medullary rays and a pretty grain; hard, close-grained, works easily.

Hydrangea vestita, Wall. *Kulain, Bh.* L. $\frac{20\text{-}30}{10\text{-}15+2\text{-}3}$ of the R. F. from 9,000 to 11,000 ft. Common all round the summit of Tongloo, 10,000 ft. Fl. 5, fr. 8-9.

Hydrangea altissima, Wall. *Sema-kúng, L.* Small tree, often climbing or epiphytic of the U. H. F. from 6,000 to 8,000 ft. Found in woods round Darjeeling. Fl. 4-5, fr. 8-9.

Dichroa febrifuga, Lour. *Basak, P.*; *Singnamook, Bh.*; *Gebokanak, L.* L. shrub E. $\frac{6\text{-}12}{0\text{-}+\frac{1}{2}\frac{1}{2}}$ of the U. H. F., from 4,000 to 8,000 ft. Fl. 7-8, fr. 12. In many forests it forms the chief undergrowth, and in open lands below 6,000 ft. is exceedingly common mixed with *Mæsa montana* and *Rubus flavus*. Bark yellow, peeling off in flakes. Wood yellowish white, hard, with fine medullary rays. The shoots and bark of the roots are made into a decoction and used as a febrifuge by the Paharias. It is a very handsome shrub, either in flower or when covered with its bright dark blue berries. Used also by Bhutias and Lepchas to burn in their religious ceremonies.

Itea macrophylla, Wall. *Teturldumm, L.* E. $\frac{30\text{-}40}{10\text{-}20+3\text{-}4}$ in L. H. F. valleys up to 4,000 ft. Fl. 5-6, fr. 11.

Ribes glaciale, Wall. *Robhay, Bh.* A shrub, often epiphytic, generally climbing, from 8,000 to 12,000 ft. Common on Tongloo. Fl. 4-5, fr. 9-10.

Note.—The black, red, and white currants, as well as the gooseberry, are occasionally cultivated in Darjeeling.

HAMAMELIDEÆ.

Bucklandia populnea, R. Br. *Pipli, P.*; *Singliang-kúng, L.* E. $\frac{60\text{-}80}{30\text{-}40+10\text{-}15}$ of the M. and U. H. F. from 3,000 to 8,000 ft. Perhaps the most ornamental of the Upper Hill trees, and one of the most valuable for timber. Fl. fr. at all seasons. Easily recognized by its thick poplar-like leaves with big fleshy conspicuous stipules. Bark brown, rough. Wood reddish brown, close-grained, hard, extensively used for planking (for which it is almost as good as Champ) beams and rafters; gives good charcoal.

RHIZOPHOREÆ.

Carallia integerrima, DC. *Palamkat, P.* E. $\frac{60\text{-}80}{20\text{-}30+6\text{-}8}$ of the M. P. F. *w.* of Terai and in L. H. F. valleys and moist forests up to 4,000 ft. Fl. 2-3. Wood reddish brown, with broad medullary rays, very heavy and close-grained, used for building purposes by Nepalese.

COMBRETACEÆ.

Terminalia belerica, Roxb. *Bahera, P.; Kanom-kúng, L.* L. $\frac{60\text{-}80}{30\text{-}40+6\text{-}8}$ of the S. F., M. P. F. *d.* of Terai and L. H. F. ridges and plateaux up to 3,000 ft. Fl. 4, fr. 12-1. Wood yellowish, hard, but not durable; rarely used except for charcoal. The kernels of the fruit are eaten.

Terminalia Chebula, Retz. *Harra, P.; Silim-kúng, L.* L. $\frac{40\text{-}50}{20\text{-}30+3\text{-}4}$ of the S. F., M. P. F. *d.* of Terai and L. H. F. ridges and plateaux up to 3,000 ft. Not so common as the former. Fl. 4, fr. 12-1. Wood yellow, hard, better than that of *T. belerica*; rarely used except for charcoal. The kernels of the fruit are eaten. The fruits are used as a medicine for sore-throat by the Paharias, who call it "Koki."

Teminalia tomentosa, W. and A. *Saj, P.; Taksor-kúng, L.* L. $\frac{80\text{-}100}{40\text{-}50+6\text{-}12}$ of the S. F. in Terai and (chiefly) in L. H. F. especially in moist places, though often found even on dry ridges. Fl. 8, fr. 2. The wood is black-brown, very hard, and strong if well seasoned. Liable to warp and split very much if cut green. It seems difficult to season, sleepers cut out of logs which had been more than one year warped exceedingly. It is used extensively for house-building, tea factories, &c. Bark greyish black, with deep vertical fissures and smaller horizontal ones, making small prominent squares. The root wood is very hard, and is used occasionally for "kukri" handles.

Terminalia myriopteron, Kurz. *Panisaj, P.; Sunglock-kúng, L.* E. $\frac{100\text{-}120}{50\text{-}60+12\text{-}20}$ or even greater girth. In the valuation survey of the Sivoke Hills in 1873-74 three trees of over 21 ft. girth (14 cubits) were reported. Found in the L. and M. H. F., in the deep valleys of the former, and constantly in the latter, up to 5,000 ft. altitude. A very handsome tree when in full flower or fruit, with its pendent boughs loaded with pink flowers or yellow seeds. The heartwood like that of saj, and used for similar purposes, but much lighter in colour, and having bands of all shades of brown and black; the sapwood is white, not broad. It is very much used in the Lower Hills for house-building and tea-boxes, and also makes very good charcoal. The bark is greyish brown, peeling off in vertical flakes, and easily recognized from that of saj.

COMBRETUM DECANDRUM, Roxb. *Kali-lara, P.*; *Pindik, L.* Large climbing shrub of S. F. and M. P. F. *d.* and *w.* in Terai and L. H. F. up to 2,000 ft. Stem cylindrical, often very big. Bark greyish white, corky. Wood brown, rather light, with numerous fine medullary rays. The young shoots have generally a delicate lilac tinge. Fl. 1-3, fr. 3-6.

COMBRETUM SQUAMOSUM, Roxb. Climbing shrub of the banks of streams in the Lower Terai. Fl. 1, fr. 4.

COMBRETUM (SARCOPTERUM, Thw.). *Sunglokvar-rik, L.* Climbing, or rather straggling, shrub of the Terai and L. Hills up to 5,000 ft. Fl. 5, fr. 10-12. Common in waste places and old cultivations.

MYRTACEÆ.

PSIDIUM GUAVA, Raddi. *Amrut, H.*; *Amuk, P.* E. $\frac{20\text{-}30}{0\text{-}10+1\text{-}2}$. Cultivated in the Terai and Lower Hills. Often found apparently wild, *e.g.* in the Bamunpokri plantation.

EUGENIA JAMBOS, Linn. E. $\frac{20\text{-}30}{10\text{-}15+2\text{-}3}$. Cultivated in the Terai. (In *Brandis' Forest Flora* it is said to be indigenous to the Sikkim Terai.)

EUGENIA JAMBOLANA, Lam. *Jaman, P.*; *Phober-kúng, L.* L. $\frac{40\text{-}60}{20\text{-}30+4\text{-}6}$ of the S. F. of the Terai and L. H. F. up to 2,000 ft. Fl. 3, fr. 7. Wood reddish brown, hard, close-grained, resembling Sâl, especially in cross section, except that it is of a rather different colour, but said to be brittle and to warp easily. The fruit is black, eaten.

The variety *E. caryophyllæfolia*, Lam., is found in the L. H.F. up to 3,000 ft., and is distinct in appearance.

EUGENIA OBOVATA, Wall. *Kiamoni, P.*; *Jungsong-kúng, L.* E. $\frac{30\text{-}40}{20\text{-}20+3\text{-}4}$ of the S. F. and Sv. F. in Terai, and on dry ridges in the L. H. F., but scarce. Very common as a small gnarled, twisted tree in Savannahs. Fruit black, eaten. Fl. 5, fr. 7. Bark, white, smooth. Wood said to be good, heavy and strong, but not used, the tree being only of small size. The bark, ground up, is said to be used by Paharias to stop headache; it is used like smelling-salts.

EUGENIA FORMOSA, Wall. *Bara Jaman, P.*; *Famsikól, L.* E. $\frac{30\text{-}40}{10\text{-}20+4\text{-}5}$ of the M. P. F. *w.* and banks of streams in Terai and L. H. F. valleys. Fl. 4., often 2 in. across and very handsome. Bark grey-white, smooth, thin. Wood hard, close-grained, rather lighter coloured than that of the Jaman, and not reddish; heavy, but not used.

EUGENIA RAMOSISSIMA, Wall. *Jamu, P.* E. $\frac{40\text{-}60}{20\text{-}30+3\text{-}5}$ of the M. P. F. *w.* in Terai and L. H. F. up to 3,000 ft. Fl. 3, fr. 6.

EUGENIA LANCEÆFOLIA, Roxb. $\frac{E}{L}$(?) $\frac{40\text{-}60}{20\text{-}30+3\text{-}5}$ of the M. P. F. *w.* in Terai (common in Dalka Jhar, especially near rivers,) and in L. H. F. valleys. Fl. 1.

EUGENIA CLAVIFLORA, Roxb. *Jumu, P., Mantet-kúng, L.* E. tree or large shrub of the L. H. F. up to 4,000 ft. Fl. 4.

EUGENIA BALSAMEA, Wight. *Archal, P.* E. $\frac{10\text{-}20}{0\cdot5+\frac{1}{2}\text{-}1}$. Common in M. P. F. in swampy places and along rivers in the Terai (*e.g.* Dalka Jhar). Fl. 11, fr. 12-1.

EUGENIA TODDALIÆFOLIA, Wight. *Sungnem-kúng, L.* E. small tree of the hill forests about 3,000 to 4,000 ft. Fl. 11.

EUGENIA CERASIFLORA, Kz. *Jaman, P.*; *Sunom-kúng, L.* E. $\frac{40\text{-}80}{20\text{-}30+4\text{-}6}$. Common tree in the M. H. F. from 3,000 to 6,000 ft.; chiefly in moist places. Fl. 10-11, fr. 2-3. Wood white, hard, close-grained, not used. Bark yellowish white, thin.

EUGENIA (PRÆCOX, Roxb.). *Chumlani, P.*; *Sunúm-kúng, L.* E. $\frac{60\text{-}80}{30\text{-}40+4\text{-}8}$ of the M. and U. H. F. from 4,000 to 6,000 ft. Very common in Sepoydura forest above Kurseong. Fl. 12, fr. 3. Wood said to be good; used occasionally for building and for the handles of tools, but more often for charcoal.

NOTE.—There are several other species, but I have only mentioned those I know well and have got named.

CAREYA ARBOREA, Roxb. *Kumbi, P.*; *Boktok-kúng, L.* L. $\frac{40\text{-}60}{20\text{-}30+4\text{-}6}$ of the S. F., Sv. F. and M. P. F. *d.* of Terai and L. H. F., especially plateaux (like Bamunpokri Hill). Fl. 4, fr. 7. Very common as a small gnarled tree in Savannahs, and as a tall big tree in the other forests. Wood dark red, close and even-grained, rather light, works very easily and would make good furniture, but is rarely used except for charcoal. Is being tried for sleepers. Bark grey-brown, falling off in small rectangular scales; inner bark red, fibrous, occasionally used for rough cords.

CAREYA HERBACEA, Roxb. *Chuwa, P.* A small shrub or perennial herb of the Sâl forests, flowering in April, coming up best after jungle fires.

NOTE.—Several other Myrtaceæ are cultivated in the district, *e.g. Myrtus communis*, L., and *Rhodomyrtus*, about Darjeeling; *Eucalyptus globulus*, Labill, at Rangbi, Rungyrúm, and many tea estates, but it does not thrive well. *Barringtonia acutangula*, Gaertn., I have seen at Julpigori; it probably may also be found in the Terai.

MELASTOMACEÆ.

MELASTOMA MALABATHRICUM, Linn. *Choulisy, P.*; *Tungbram-kúng, L.* E. $\frac{5\text{-}15}{0\cdot4+\frac{1}{2}\text{-}\frac{3}{4}}$ of the Terai, chiefly near streams in open ground and Lower Hills, up to 6,000 ft. Fl. 4, fr. 11.

OXYSPORA PANICULATA, Wall. E. $\frac{10\text{-}15}{0\cdot5+\frac{1}{2}\text{-}1}$ of the M. H. F. from 4,000 to 6,000 ft. Very handsome shrub. Fl. 8, fr. 1.

OSBECKIA STELLATA, Don. *Number-kúng, L.* L. $\frac{6\text{-}10}{0+\frac{1}{2}\text{-}\frac{3}{4}}$. Shrub common in M. and U. H. F. from 4,000 to 8,000 ft. Very pretty shrub, common in Darjeeling. Fl. 7, fr. 10.

OSBECKIA CRINITA, Bth. Shrub of the L. and M. H. F. from 2,000 to 6,000 ft. Has very large handsome red flowers. Fl. 9-10.

Osbeckia angustifolia, Don. Tall shrub, very common in Savannah lands and near streams in the Terai, where it is very conspicuous. Fl. 9-12.

Note.—*Osbeckia Nepalensis*, Hook., with red or white flowers, is common in ditches and swampy places in Terai and Lower Hills; *Osbeckia* (*nutans*, Wall.) on rocks in the Lower Hills, *e.g.* on the cart-road between Sukna and Chunbati; and *Osbeckia Chinensis*, Willd., in fields and grassy forests in the southern Terai.

LYTHRACEÆ.

Woodfordia floribunda, Salisb. *Dahiri, P.*; *Chungkyekdúm, L.* Large shrub of the hill sides of the Tista valley. Fl. 3. (A variety of this I have found in the Tista Valley growing to a tree $\frac{40}{20+3-4}$.)

Lawsonia alba, Lam. *Mehndi, H.* A shrub occasionally found in cultivation in the Terai.

Lagerstrœmia parviflora, Roxb. *Sida, M.*; *Borderi, P.*; *Borodengri, P.*; *Kunhil-kúng, L.* L. $\frac{60-80}{30-50+6-8}$ of the S. F., Sv. F., M. P. F. *d.* of Terai and L. H. F. up to 3,000 ft. Fl. 5, fr. 8-12. Wood light brown, smooth, even-grained, with large pores; used occasionally for house-building and makes good charcoal. Bark grey-white, peeling off in large flakes, is easily recognized in forest. As a small tree it is very common in mixed forests, and as a large one in Sâl forests, and especially in the Lower Hills (*e.g.* the upper plateau at Bamunpokri). It is very quick-growing, either from seed or coppice shoots.

Duabanga sonneratoides, Buch. *Lampatia, P.*; *Door-kúng, L.* E L (?) $\frac{80-100}{30-40+8-16}$ or perhaps even greater girth. Found in L. H. F. especially by the side of rivers, and up to 3,000 ft., occasionally in S. F. and M. P. F. in Terai. Fl. 1, fr. 3-4. One of the handsomest trees in the district, with its long pendent boughs with opposite leaves and large terminal flowers. Bark light brown, peeling off in small thin flakes. Wood valuable for many purposes, and of late years more employed than any other low-level tree, except perhaps "toon." It is grey-brown, with rings of different shades of brown and yellow, smooth, with a satiny lustre; it is used for beams, planking, tea-boxes, &c.; it is one of the best woods for dug-outs, as it is not liable to warp, and is used by Paharias for cattle-troughs.

Punica granatum, Linn. *Anar, H.* The pomegranate. Small tree, occasionally cultivated in Terai and Hills, up to 4,000 ft. Fl. 3.

SAMYDACEÆ.

Casearia glomerata, Roxb. *Burgonli, P.*; *Sugvat-kúng, L.* E. $\frac{40-60}{20-30+6-8}$ in the M. and U. H. F. from 4,000 to 7,000 ft. In old cultivated lands comes up very often with *Mœsa*, *Saurauja*, &c., but is generally small; in forests it becomes a big tree. Fl. 3, fr. 6.

Wood yellowish white, hard, close-grained, with numerous fine medullary rays. Used for building purposes, charcoal, &c.

CASEARIA HAMILTONII, Wall. *Tanki-kúng, L.* L. $\frac{30\text{-}40}{15\text{-}20+4\text{-}5}$ of the L. H. F. up to 3,000 ft. Fl. ?, fr. 4.

CASEARIA VARECA, Roxb. L. $\frac{15\text{-}20}{0\text{-}5+\frac{1}{2}\text{-}1}$ of the M. P. F. *w.* and banks of streams in Terai and in L. H. F. valleys. Fl. ?, fr. 1.

CASEARIA SP. E. $\frac{15\text{-}20}{0\text{-}5+\frac{1}{2}\text{-}1}$. Small tree of the M. H. F., chiefly of old cultivations, with big leaves and big yellow fruit. Fr. 8.

PASSIFLOREÆ.

CARICA PAPAYA, Linn. *Papoi*; *Papita.* Cultivated all over the Terai.

DATISCEÆ.

TETRAMELES NUDIFLORA, R. Br. *Maina-kat, P.*; *Payomko-kúng, L.* L. $\frac{100\text{-}120}{50\text{-}80+10\text{-}20}$ and perhaps even of greater size. Found in the L. H. F. up to 3,000 ft., and occasionally in M. P. F. in Terai. Very fast-growing. Fl. 4, fr. 5-6. Wood soft, not used; might be tried for tea-boxes. Bark light brown, scaly. The stem is generally very straight and cylindrical above, often much buttressed below. There is one on the Tista valley road, near the Ruyem Jhora, which, though not measured, cannot be less than 150 ft. high, with a girth of 30 ft. or more. It is, however, very deeply buttressed. There is another enormous one in the Chenga valley.

ARALIACEÆ.

ARALIA NOLIOLOSA. *Somri, P.*; *Kajyang-kúng, L.* E. $\frac{20\text{-}30}{18\text{-}28+1\text{-}2}$ small tree of the M. H. F. from 3,000 to 5,000 ft. Stem covered with prickles. Fl. 1, fr. ? Very handsome; has somewhat the appearance of a tree-fern.

ARALIA . *Somri, P.*; *Kajyang-kúng, L.* E. $\frac{20\text{-}30}{18\text{-}28+1\text{-}2}$ in similar places; differs in having much larger leaves and fewer prickles. Fl. 6, fr. 7-8.

PENTAPANAX LESCHENAULTII, Seem. *Tungshing, Bh.* L. $\frac{30\text{-}40}{15\text{-}20+3\text{-}4}$ of the U. H. F. and R. F. from 7,000 to 11,000 ft. Common in Tongloo. Fl. ?, fr. 10.

PENTAPANAX SUBCORDATUM, Seem. *Mandani*; *Singhatta, P.*; *Siriokhytem-kúng, L.* Big climber of the U. H. F. from 5,000 to 8,000 ft. Common round Darjeeling. Fl. fr. 5-6.

Pentapanax racemosum, Seem. *Ballera, P.*; *Prongzamnyok, L.* Very big climber of the U. H. F. from 6,000 to 8,000 ft. Common about Darjeeling, and easily recognized by its racemose inflorescence. Fl. 4-5, fr. 5-6.

Helwingia Himalaica, Hk. f. and T. *Lubbor-kúng, L.* Shrub of the U. H. F. from 7,000 to 8,000 ft. Common about Senchal. Fl. 5, fr. 7-8. Recognized by the flowers being clustered on the middle of the midrib of the leaf, like those of *Ruscus.*

Heptapleurum (elatum, Seem). *Chinia, P.*; *Prongzam-kúng, L.* E. $\frac{40-50}{20-30+4-5}$ of the U. H. F. from 5,000 to 7,000 ft. Fl. 10, fr. 12.

Heptapleurum (glaucum, Bth. and Hk. f.) *Chinia, P.*; *Hloprongzam-kúng, L.* E. $\frac{40-50}{20-30+4-5}$ of the U. H. F. from 6,000 to 8,000 ft. Fl. fr. most seasons. The soft young leaves are eaten by Lepchas.

Heptapleurum tomentosum, Ham. *Baloo Chinia, P.*; *Suntong-kúng, L.* E. $\frac{50-60}{20-30+4-5}$ of the U. H. F. and R. F. from 6,000 to 10,000 ft. Common on Tongloo. Fl. 5-7, fr. 9-11. Wood white, soft, shining, not used.

Heptapleurum venulosum, Seem. *Singhata-lara, P.* Large straggling shrub or climber of L. and M. H. F. from 3,000 to 5,000 ft. Fl. 12-1, fr. 2-3.

Trevesia palmata, Vis. *Kajpati, P.*; *Suntong-kúng, L.* E. $\frac{10-15}{5-10+\frac{1}{2}-1}$ of the M. P. F. *w.* and banks of streams in Terai and L. H. F. valleys up to 3,000 ft. Fl. 4, fr. 5. Fruit eaten by Lepchas.

Heteropanax fragrans, Seem. *Lal Totilla, P.*; *Siriokhtem-kúng, L.* E. $\frac{10-20}{8-18+1-2}$ of the Terai, M. P. F. *d.* and occasionally S. F.; also L. H. F. ridges and dry exposures. Fl. 12-1, fr. 4. The Pahari name is from its resemblance to *Calosanthes.*

Brassaiopsis hamla, Ham. *Tilhetter, P.*; *Sungtong-kúng, L.* E. $\frac{20-30}{5-10+2-3}$ of the L. and M. H. F. valleys from 1,000 to 4,000 ft. Fl. 2-3, fr. 5. Much branched. Fine specimens may be seen on the zigzags of the road from Pankabari to Kurseong. Leaves used for fodder.

Brassaiopsis hispida, Seem. *Phota, P.*; *Sungtong-kúng, L.* L. (?) $\frac{15-20}{5-10+\frac{1}{2}-1}$. Small tree of U. H. F. from 5,000 to 7,000 ft. Fl. 2.

Brassaiopsis . *Moqchini, P.*; *Sungtong-kúng, L.* L. $\frac{20-30}{5-10+1-2}$ of the U. H. F. from 6,000 to 8,000 ft. The commonest one about Darjeeling, and remarkable for its handsome palmatifid leaves. Fl. 7-8. The fruit is eaten by Lepchas. Wood white, soft, with numerous medullary rays, shining. Leaves used for fodder.

Brassaiopsis floribunda, Seem. Tree of the U. H. F. about 6,000 to 7,000 ft. Fl. fr. 4-6.

MACROPANAX UNDULATUM, Seem. *Chinia, P.*; *Prongzam-kúng, L.* E. $\frac{20\text{-}30}{10\text{-}15+2\text{-}3}$ of the L. and M. H. F. up to 5,000 ft. Fl. 8, fr. 12.

HEDERA HELIX, Linn. *Dudela-lara, P.* E. climber of the U. H F., 6,000 to 7,000 ft., but rare. Fl. 8-9, fr. 10-11. Cultivated about Darjeeling. (I have not seen them, but the wild plant is said to have red berries.)

NOTE.—There are several other species of *Araliaceæ* besides, which require investigation and names.

CORNACEÆ.

MARLEA BEGONIÆFOLIA, Roxb. *Paletnyok, L.* (in U. Hills.); *Palet-kúng, L.* (L. Hills and Terai); *Timil, P.* Small tree. L. $\frac{20\text{-}30}{10\text{-}15+2\text{-}3}$. Perhaps the widest ranging of the trees in the district, as it is found from the Terai up to 9,000 ft. In the Terai it is chiefly found in waste lands and in the tangled thickets on the banks of rivers. Fl. 6, fr. 8. Wood white, close-grained, not used.

CORNUS MACROPHYLLA, Wall. *Patmoro, P.* Small tree, not common, 3,000 to 6,000 ft. Fl. 5-6, fr. .

CORNUS CAPITATA, Wall. *Tumbuk, L.* Tree L. $\frac{40\text{-}60}{20\text{-}30+4\text{-}5}$, 6,000 to 8,000 ft. Not very common. Very handsome when in full flower, with its large cream-coloured bracts. Fine specimens may be seen near the 18th mile of the cart-road, close to Darjeeling, and on the Auckland road. Fl. 5, fr. 7. Wood white, very hard, close-grained; has been tried as a substitute for boxwood.

AUCUBA HIMALAICA, Hk. f. and T. *Singne, L.*; *Tapathyer, L.*; *Phul Amphi, P.* L. shrub or small tree. E. $\frac{10\text{-}20}{0\text{-}6+1\text{-}2}$ of U. H. F. from 5,000 to 9,000 ft. Diœcious. Fl. 4-5, fr. 9-10. Bark greyish brown, smooth. Heartwood dark grey-brown, black when freshly cut; sapwood grey. Medullary rays very numerous, of all sizes. Annual rings marked by a line of pores. A specimen examined had 45 rings to a mean radius of 2¼ in. Wood heavy, hard.

TORRICELLIA TILIÆFOLIA, DC. Small tree of U. H. F. 6,000 to 10,000 ft. Fl. 5-6, fr. 8.

CAPRIFOLIACEÆ.

PENTAPYXIS STIPULATA, Hk. f. *Berikuru, P.* Large straggling shrub, exceedingly common round Darjeeling. Fl. 4, fr. 6. Wood white, hard, close-grained, with numerous fine medullary rays, and often with a greenish tinge.

LONICERA GLABRATA, Wall. *Bet-lara, P.* Climbing shrub, 5,000 to 7,000 ft. Common round Darjeeling. Fl. 8-9, fr. 11. Sweet-scented. Wood brown, soft.

LONICERA JAPONICA, Thunb. *Duari-lara, P.* Climbing shrub 4,000 to 10,000 ft. Distinguished from the former by its very long corolla tube and soft leaves. Fl. 6, fr. .

LONICERA GRACILIS. Shrub. Not common, only found once by me, viz. at Laba, near Dumsong, 6,000 ft. Fl. ?, fr. 4.

LEYCESTERIA FORMOSA, Wall. *Tunguk-kúng, L.* Shrub with hollow stems and glaucous leaves. Common about Darjeeling, 7,000 ft. Fl. 6, fr. 8.

VIBURNUM ERUBESCENS, Wall. *Ganné, P.*; *Kancha-kúng, L.*; *Damshíng, Bh.* Small tree. L. $\frac{10\text{-}20}{2\text{-}5+1\text{-}2}$, 6,000 to 10,000 ft. altitude. Common in forest of second growth. Fl. 4-5, fr. 6-7. Has many varieties. Wood pinkish white, hard, close-grained, heavy, a little resembling boxwood; would possibly do for wood-carving if well dried and seasoned. Only used by Paharias for house posts.

VIBURNUM CORYLIFOLIUM, Hk. f. and T. Tree $\frac{20\text{-}30}{5\text{-}15+2\text{-}3}$, 8,000 to 10,000 ft. altitude. Found on Sundukpho. Fl. ?, fr. 10.

VIBURNUM INVOLUCRATUM, Wall. *Gorakuri, P.* Small tree or L. shrub of 6,000 to 8,000 ft. Very handsome in full flower. Fl. 7, fr. ? Found on Senchal.

VIBURNUM CORIACEUM, Bl. *Gorakuri, P.* (*bara*). Small tree. E. $\frac{20\text{-}30}{5\text{-}10+1\text{-}2}$. Common in hills from 4,000 to 8,000 ft. Seeds give an oil, which is extracted by the Paharias and used both for food and to burn. Fl. 8, fr. 12.

VIBURNUM PUNCTATUM, Ham. Shrub, 3,000 to 5,000 ft. Not common. Fl. 8, fr. 10. Much resembling the last.

VIBURNUM LUTESCENS, Bl. Forests of Terai and Lower Hills. L., 2,000 ft. in valleys. L. shrub $\frac{6\text{-}10}{0+\frac{1}{2}\text{-}1}$. Fl. 1-2, fr. 10. Common at Sivoke and in the Dalka Jhar.

SAMBUCUS ADNATA, Wall. *Chiriyabaug, P.* Shrub, 7,000 to 10,000 ft.

SAMBUCUS JAVANICA, Reinw. *Galeni, P.* L. shrub or small tree $\frac{20\text{-}30}{0+2\text{-}3}$. Common in second-growth forest, from 4,000 to 8,000 ft. Wood rather soft, white, with numerous fine medullary rays.

RUBIACEÆ.

ANTHOCEPHALUS CADAMBA, Bth. and Hk. f. *Kadam, P.*; *Pandoor-kúng, L.* L. $\frac{40\text{-}60}{20\text{-}30+4\text{-}8}$ of the M. P. F. of Terai and L. H. F. up to 3,000 ft. Fl. 7. Wood yellow, light, has occasionally been tried for tea-boxes, &c. Very quick growing.

STEPHEGYNE SP. *Kalé, P.*; *Kalikat, P.* Large tree of the L. H. F. Not very common. Wood bright orange-yellow, with pores of darker colour, rather heavy, close-grained. Sapwood of rather lighter colour, often pink; used for planking and other building purposes.

ADINA CORDIFOLIA, Hk. f. and Bth. *Karam, P.*; *Numbong-kúng, L.* E. $\frac{40\text{-}60}{20\text{-}30+6\text{-}8}$ of the M. F. P. *d.* in Terai and L. H. F.

up to 2,000 ft. Fl. 8. Wood yellow, heavy, close-grained; much used for building in the Terai, and in great demand. The tree is very rare east of the Balasan river, but common to the west, in the Balasan, Chenga, and Lohagarhi forests.

UNCARIA PILOSA, Bth. *Baisi kara, P.*; *Kahuk-rig, L.* A large straggling shrub of the L. H. F. up to 3,000 ft. Fl. 4. It has a pair of large recurved stipules, like buffalo horns, whence the native name.

UNCARIA SESSILIFRUCTUS, Roxb. *Kali-kara, P.*; *Pinri, L.* Large climbing shrub of the L. H. F. and inner valleys up to 4,000 ft. Fl. 11, fr. 12-1.

CINCHONA SUCCIRUBRA, Pavon. The species of cinchona chiefly cultivated in the Rungbi plantation, in the Pomong Association's Garden and for ornament at Kodabari, Selim, and elsewhere.

CINCHONA CALISAYA, Weddell. Also cultivated in the Rungbi plantation.

CINCHONA OFFICINALIS, L. Has been tried at the Rungbi plantation, where specimens may be seen close to the inspection bungalow, but is not generally cultivated.

CINCHONA MICRANTHA, Ruiz et Pavon. This has also been tried, but I believe is not now cultivated.

NOTE.—There are several other species and varieties, I believe; for an account of which, and the system of growth and manufacture, reference may be made to the Government reports and to the *Manual of Cinchona Cultivation in India* by Dr. King, Superintendent of the Royal Botanical Garden, Calcutta.

HYMENOPOGON PARASITICUS, Wall. *Kursimla, P.* Epiphytic small shrub of the M. and U. H. F. from 5,000 to 8,000 ft. Fl. 5, fr. 11. Flowers white, with white bracts.

HYMENODICTYON THYRSIFLORUM, Wall. L. $\frac{30\text{-}50}{20\text{-}30+4\text{-}6}$ of the S. F., Sv. F. and M. P. F. *d.* of Terai and L. H. F. (scarce). Common in some Savannahs, as at Mohurgong and Champasari, and in the southern S. F., like the Tehsilpur Jhar. Bark brownish grey, corky. Wood soft, white, not used.

HYMENODICTYON FLACCIDUM, Wall. Tree of the L. and M. H. F. up to 5,000 ft. Not very common.

LUCULIA GRATISSIMA, Sweet. *Dowari, P.*; *Simbran-grip, L.* Large shrub or small tree of the M. H. F. about 4,000 to 6,000 ft. Fl. 10-11. Has very handsome pink long-tubed flowers, which the Paharias and Lepchas, men and women, are fond of wearing. Leaves used in dyeing.

WENDLANDIA CINEREA, DC. *Tilki, P.*; *Mimri, P.* E. $\frac{20\text{-}30}{10\text{-}15+2\text{-}3}$ of the L. H. F., and occasionally in Sv. F. in Terai, but only close to the hills. Very common at Choklong and in the Chenga forest, where in winter its very light-coloured foliage makes the tree very conspicuous. Fl. 4. Bark brown, with numerous vertical fissures.

WENDLANDIA (CORIACEA DC.) *Tilgia, P.* E. $\frac{20\text{-}30}{10\text{-}15+2\text{-}3}$ of the M. P. F. and L. H. F. Fl. 2-3. Common on the Singari Pahar ridge, south of Sivoke. Has lanceolate leaves.

WENDLANDIA EXSERTA, DC. *Kangi, P.* Tree of the S. F. and M. P. F. in Terai and L. H. F. Fl. 3.

WENDLANDIA SP. *Kangi, P.*; *Singnok, L.* Common tree of the L. and M. H. F. from 2,000 to 5,000 ft. Fl. 2.

HEDYOTIS CAPITELLATA, Wall. *Bakre-lara, P.*; *Kulhenyok, L.* E. soft-wooded climber of Terai, L. and M. H. F. up to 6,000 ft. Used by the Lepchas as a green dye. The green leaves are put in water and infused, and the cloth to be dyed steeped in the infusion. The Paharias also use it mixed with leaves of *Luculia* as a blue dye. It seems to be more as a mordant that it is used than as a regular dye. Leaves eaten by Lepchas.

MUSSÆNDA MACROPHYLLA, Wall. *Asari, P.*; *Tumberh-kúng, L.* Large shrub or small tree of the M. H. F. from 4,000 to 6,000 ft. Fl. 6-8, fr. 9. Flowers orange, calyx with one yellow-white leaf-like lobe.

MUSSÆNDA FRONDOSA, Willd. *Asari, P.*; *Tumberh-kúng, L.* Large shrub of the L. and M. H. F. from the Terai up to 4,000 ft. Fl. 6-8, fr. 9. Flowers orange, calyx with one yellow-white leaf-like lobe.

ADENOSACME LONGIFOLIA, Wall. *Pitamari, P.* Shrub of the L. H. F., damp, and M. H. F., up to 6,000 ft. Fl. 6, fr. 11. Berries snow-white.

RANDIA DUMETORUM, Lam. *Amuki, P.*; *Maidal, P.*; *Gundrow, M.*; *Panji-kúng, L.* E. $\frac{15\text{-}20}{5\text{-}8+1\text{-}2}$ of the S. F., Sv. F. and M. P. F. *d.* in Terai and L. H. F. up to 2 000 ft. Fl. 5, fr. 1-2. Wood hard, close-grained, strong, white, with streaks of brown-green, and almost blue. Bark brown-grey, peeling off in small round flakes. Flowers rather small. Fruit about 1-1½ inches diameter. The Mechis use the fruit to kill fish.

RANDIA ULIGINOSA, DC. *Maidal, P.* E. $\frac{15\text{-}20}{5\text{-}8+1\text{-}2}$ of the S. F. and Sv. F. in the Terai. Is rare in the former, but very common in, and characteristic of, Savannahs. Fl. 5, fr. 1-2. Fruit big, resembling a guava, eaten by Mechis. Flowers large, white, sweet-scented.

RANDIA (LATIFOLIA, Lam.). A very prickly shrub of the damp inner forests of the Lower Hills.

RANDIA RIGIDA, DC. E. $\frac{10\text{-}15}{0\text{-}5+1\text{-}2}$ of the L. H. F. damp inner valleys. Common in the Tista valley beyond the first bend above Sivoke. Fr. 1, small, black.

IXORA UNDULATA, Roxb. *Pari, P.*; *Takchirnyok, L.* Small tree of the L. H. F. valleys and M. P. F. *w.* in Terai. Fl. 5, fr. 7.

IXORA ACUMINATA, Roxb. *Churipat, P.* Large shrub of the L. H. F. valleys. Fl. 4, in large white heads, fragrant.

IXORA TOMENTOSA, Roxb. *Sundok-kúng, L.* L. $\frac{15\text{-}20}{5\text{-}10+1\text{-}2}$ of the S. F. and M. P. F. *d.* of Terai and L. H. F. up to 2,000 ft. Fl. 5-6, fr. 8-10.

NOTE.—*Ixora coccinea*, L., may be seen in cultivation in gardens in the Terai.

VANGUERIA SPINOSA, Roxb. A small thorny tree found along roadsides in the Lower Terai. Fl. 4, fr. 10-11, resembling a small guava.

COFFEA ARABICA, Linn. The coffee plant. Has been cultivated in the district, and in one case a company was once formed to grow it, but it is now only to be found here and there as specimens.

COFFEA BENGALENSIS, Roxb. Small shrub of the K. S. F., M. P. F. *d.* and waste places in the Terai. Fl. 2-4, white, fragrant; fr. 6-11. The berries are said to be used for coffee by the Mechis and Rajbanshis of the Terai and Western Duars.

MORINDA BRACTEATA, Roxb. *Hurdi, P.*; *Huldi-kúng, L.* Large shrub of the Terai and L. H. F. The bark of the roots of this and the next species gives the "Hurdi" dye; it gives a red or yellow colour, and is very largely exported, chiefly from the hills between the Mahanadi and Tista rivers.

MORINDA LANCEOLATA. *Dala Hurdi, P.*; *Huldi-kúng, L.* Large shrub of the S. F., M. P. F. in Terai, and L. Hills. Fl. 3-4. For use see above.

PSYCHOTRIA VIRIDIFLORA, Rwdt. *Guglat, P.*; *Den-nok, L.* Shrub reaching 4-6 ft. of the M. P. F. *w.* and L. H. F. up to 3,000 ft. Fl. 7-8, fr. 1-4. (There is another species very similar and in similar localities, probably *P. calophylla*, Wall.)

CHASALIA CURVIFLORA, Thw. *Antabi, L.* Shrub. Common in L. and M. H. F. from 2,000 ft. to 6,000 ft. Fl. 6. Leaves eaten by Lepchas.

LASIANTHUS (LUCIDUS, DC.) *Chhota Galeni, P.*; *Kalhet-kúng, L.* Small tree of the L. H. F., damp places. Fr. 1-2.

LASIANTHUS SP. . *Deomuk, L.* Common shrub of the U. H. F. from 6,000 to 9,000 ft., and round Darjeeling. Very conspicuous with its bright turquoise blue berries. Fl. 5, fr. 9.

PŒDERIA FŒTIDA, Willd. *Padebiri, P.*; *Takpœdrik, L.* Common small climbing shrub; common throughout the district, from the thickets near Siliguri to above Darjeeling. Fl. 10, fr. 12-1. Flowers red fringed, resembling those of the *Cinchonas.* The fruit is used to blacken the teeth by Lepchas and Paharias; this, they say, is as a specific against toothache.

HAMILTONIA SUAVEOLENS, Roxb. *Bainchanpa, P.* Large shrub with handsome panicles of blue-lilac flowers, found in L. H. F. with Sâl. Fl. 11. (I have only once met with it, and that in the Upper Rilli forest, east of the Tista.)

RUBIA CORDIFOLIA, Linn. *Manjit*; *Vhyem, L.* A common small climber of the M. and U. H. F. Mentioned here as it is extensively used for dyeing throughout the district, and as large quantities are annually collected for export.

NOTE.—The species of this family do not yet seem to be perfectly determined. When they are better known, a great number of other trees and shrubs will come into the list, and especially in the genera *Wendlandia, Morinda, Psychotria,* and *Lasianthus,* and many of the names here given will probably be altered.

COMPOSITÆ.

VERNONIA VOLKAMERIÆFOLIA, DC. E. $\frac{10\text{-}20}{4\text{-}5+1\text{-}2}$. Small tree of Lower Hills, up to 4,000 ft. Fl. 2-3, fr. 6-7.

CONYZA BALSAMIFERA, DC. E. $\frac{6\text{-}10}{1\text{-}2+\frac{1}{2}\text{-}\frac{1}{4}}$. Large shrub or small tree, chiefly found in old cultivation in the Terai and up to 4,000 ft.

INULA EUPATORIOIDES, DC. Shrub, chiefly found in dry places, as in ridge Sâl forests.

INULA CAPPA, DC. Shrub, chiefly of old cultivations in the Hills, at 3,000 to 6,000 ft.

ARTEMISIA VULGARIS, Linn. *Titapat, P.* Perennial herb or shrub (stems sometimes 6-8 in. girth), coming up thickly everywhere where the land has been once cleared for cultivation, and covering large tracts of land between 3,000 and 6,000 ft.

VACCINIACEÆ.

VACCINIUM OBOVATUM, Wight. *Ratay, P.* Common shrub, often epiphytic, of the U. H. F., from 7,000 to 9,000 ft. Fl. 5. Flowers pink.

VACCINIUM DUNALIANUM, Wight. Shrub, often epiphytic, of U. H. F., from 5,000 to 8,000 ft. Fl. 5. Flowers small, pink.

VACCINIUM RUGOSUM. *Muntirh, L.* Epiphytic, bulbous rooted small shrub of 6,000 to 8,000 ft. Fl. 7. Flowers yellowish white.

VACCINIUM SERRATUM, Wight. *Charu, P.* Shrub, bulbous rooted, often epiphytic, of 4,000 to 8,000 ft. Fl. 5. Flowers white. Leaves in whorls.

AGAPETES SALIGNA, Bth. Large epiphytic shrub of L. and M. H. F. from 1,000 to 5,000 ft. Fl. 3. Flowers dark red, long.

PENTAPTERYGIUM SERPENS, Bth. *Kali hurchu, P.*; *Koombooten, L.* Small shrub, bulbous rooted, sometimes on rocks, sometimes epiphytic, of the U. H. F. from 6,000 to 8,000 ft. Fl. 1-5. It is used, ground up, as a medicine for cattle to cure lameness. It seems to be applied as a poultice. Flowers crimson with black markings, long.

ERICACEÆ.

ANDROMEDA OVALIFOLIA, Wall. *Aigiri, P.*; *Piazay, Bh.*; *Kungshior, L.* L. $\frac{15\text{-}25}{5\text{-}15+2\text{-}3}$. One of the most universally distributed trees in the district, being found from the Tista Valley Sâl forests at 2,000 ft. up to Tongloo at 10,000 ft. Common about Darjeeling. Fl. 6-7, fr. 11-12. Bark brown, papery, peeling off in vertical strips. Wood said to be good, but not used.

ENKIANTHUS HIMALAICUS, Hk. f. and T. Small tree of the R. F., about 10,000 to 11,000 ft. Found in Tongloo. Fr. 10-11.

GAULTHERIA GRIFFITHIANA, Wight. Small shrub of the U. H. F., chiefly on rocks, from 7,000 to 9,000 ft. Fl. 7.

NOTE.—*G. repens*, Bth., is a little wiry trailing shrub found on rocks about Darjeeling and up to 12,000 ft. Fl. 10-11.

RHODODENDRON ARBOREUM, Sm. *Lal guras, P.*; *Etok, Bh.*; *Etok, L.* E. $\frac{20\text{-}30}{5\text{-}15+3\text{-}5}$ of the U. H. F. and R. F. from 6,000 to 11,000 ft. It is chiefly common in Tongloo, but good trees are found in the Senchal, Gumpahar, and Dumsong forests. Wild as well as cultivated in Darjeeling. Fl. 3-4, fr. 10. Bark pink-brown, peeling off in flakes, leaving the red inner layers exposed. Wood pink-white, hard, close-grained; used for kukri handles, small boxes, etc., and for fuel, for which it is excellent. The flowers are used to adorn temples in Sikkim; they are pink or light crimson coloured.

RHODODENDRON ARGENTEUM, Hk. f. *Kali guras, P.*; *Etok-amat, L.* E. $\frac{30\text{-}50}{10\text{-}20+3\text{-}5}$ of the U. H. F. and R. F. from 6,000 to 9,000 ft. Common below Tongloo, but not on the summit. Also common in the forests of Senchal and Gumpahar, and on all the ridges of the Dumsong Hills. Wild as well as cultivated in Darjeeling. Fl. 3-4, fr. 10. Bark red-brown, peeling off in small scales. Flowers pure white, with purple inside at the base of the corolla. Leaves large, silvery beneath. It is generally the earliest species to flower.

RHODODENDRON FALCONERI, Hk. f. *Kégoo, Bh.* E. $\frac{20\text{-}40}{10\text{-}20+2\text{-}3}$ of the R. F. and F. F. above 8,000 ft. Very common about Tongloo. Fl. 4-5, fr. 11-12. Bark purple-red beneath, outer bark red-brown, peeling off in flakes. Flowers cream-white. Leaves large, with dense rusty tomentum beneath.

RHODODENDRON BARBATUM, Wall. *Guras, P.*; *Kemoo, Bh.* E. $\frac{15\text{-}20}{5\text{-}10+2\text{-}3}$ of the R. F. from 8,000 to 11,000 ft. Common on Tongloo and the whole Singalila range. Fl. 2-3, fr. 10. Bark purple-red, peeling off in flakes. Flowers deep crimson. Leaves green, not silvery beneath.

RHODODENDRON CAMPBELLIÆ, Hk. f. Tree of the R. F. and F. F. above 10,000 ft. Recognized by its leaves having an orange-coloured down beneath, but otherwise like those of *R. arboreum*.

RHODODENDRON FULGENS, Hk. f. *Chimal, P.* Small tree or large shrub, common in Sundukpho, 11,000 ft. Fl. crimson (?) 5, fr. 10.

RHODODENDRON HODGSONI, Hk. f. E. $\frac{10\text{-}15}{0\text{-}5+\frac{1}{2}\text{-}1}$ of the undergrowth of F. F. and open places above 10,000 ft. Does not occur before Sundukpho. Fl. 5, fr. 10-11. Leaves resembling those of *R. argenteum*. Flowers pink-lilac.

RHODODENDRON CINNABARINUM, Hk. f. *Booloo, P.* E. $\frac{5\text{-}15}{0\text{-}5+\frac{1}{2}\text{-}1}$ of the high ridges, very common on Sundukpho. Fl. 4-5, fr. 10. Wood yellow-brown, close-grained, hard. Leaves poisonous.

RHODODENDRON LANATUM, Hk. f. *Chimal, P.* Small tree of the high ridges about Suburkum and Phalut. Fr. 10.

RHODODENDRON LEPIDOTUM, Wall. Small shrub, covering the rocks about Sundukpho. Fl. 8-10.

RHODODENDRON VACCINIOIDES, Hk. f. Small shrub, common in the U. H. F. about 7,000 to 8,000 ft. Fl. 6-7. Common at Rungbool.

RHODODENDRON DALHOUSIÆ, Hk. f. *Guras, P.* Shrub, often epiphytic, 6-10 ft. high, of the U. H. F. from 6,000 to 8,000 ft. Fl. 6-7; flowers very large, cream-coloured, sweet-scented.

RHODODENDRON EDGEWORTHII, Hk. f. Shrub, often epiphytic, 4-6 ft. high, of the U. H. F. from 7,000 to 8,000 ft. Fl. 8-9. Large, pure white, sweet-scented.

NOTE.—In Sikkim there are many other species, many specimens of which I have received from Mr. C. B. Clarke, M.A., Education Department, such as *R. campanulatum*, Don, 11,000 ft., mauve flowers; *R. Wightii*, Hk. f., 11,500 ft., light yellow flowers; *R. pendulum*, Hk. f., 10,000 ft.; *R. glaucum*, Hk. f., 10,000 ft.; *R. Maddeni*, Hk. f., 11,000 ft.; *R. Thomsoni*, Hk. f., 10,000 ft.; *R. ciliatum*, Hk. f., 10,000 ft.; *R. Griffithianum*, Wight, 8,000 ft.; *R. pumilum*, Hk. f., 13,000 ft.; *R. virgatum*, Hk. f., 11,000 ft.; *R. Edgarii*, C. B. C., 11,000 ft.—making 24 species in British and Independent Sikkim.

MYRSINACEÆ.

MÆSA INDICA, A. DC. *Bilauni, P.*; *Purmo-kúng, L.* E. $\frac{4\text{-}20}{0\text{-}4+\frac{1}{4}\text{-}2}$ of the Terai, L. M. and U. H. F. up to 6,000 ft. Fl. fr. at various seasons. Many varieties. (If *M. montana*, A. DC., is separate, then the common shrub or small tree of the hillsides is probably *montana*, and the small round or long deeply-serrate leaved one of the Terai and L. H. F., with short racemes, *Indica*.) Probably, except *Artemisia*, the commonest woody plant in the district, as it is everywhere met with between 3,000 and 6,000 ft. In some places, especially abandoned cultivations, it forms a small coppice-like dense forest, almost alone. The wood is rather hard, close-grained, white, with fine medullary rays.

MÆSA SP. E. $\frac{10\text{-}15}{0\text{-}5+\frac{1}{2}\text{-}1}$. A shrub or small tree of the U. H. F. about 6,000 ft. I have only seen it in grassy glades on the Laba-Dalingkot road. Fl. 3.

MÆSA MACROPHYLLA, Wall. *Bogoti, P.*; *Tugom-kúng, L.* E. $\frac{15\text{-}20}{0\text{-}10+1\text{-}2}$ of the L. H. F. and old cultivations, up to 5,000 ft. Fl. 5, fr. 10

MYRSINE SEMISERRATA, Wall. *Bilauni, P.*; *Tungcheong-kúng, L.* E. $\frac{20\text{-}30}{10\text{-}15+3\text{-}4}$ of the M. and U. H. F. from 4,000 to 8,000 ft. Fl. fr. 12-3. Wood said to be hard and good.

SAMARA FRONDOSA, King. nov. sp. *Amili-lara, P.*; *Monk-yourig, L.* Climber of the U. H. F. from 6.000 to 8,000 ft. Fl. 5, fr. 9. Bark thick, spongy. Wood soft, with large pores and very broad medullary rays. Leaves eaten by Bhutias.

EMBELIA RIBES, Burm. *Himalchiri, P.* E. climber of the M. P. F. *w.* in Terai and L. H. F. up to 4,000 ft. Fl. 11-12, fr. 4.

EMBELIA ROBUSTA, Roxb. *Kalay Bogoti, P.* E. $\frac{10\text{-}15}{0\text{-}5+\frac{1}{2}\text{-}1}$. Small tree or straggling shrub of S. F. and M. P. F. *d.* in Terai and L. H. valleys. Fl. ?, fr. 10-11. Seeds eaten by Paharias.

EMBELIA FLORIBUNDA, Wall. *Himalchiri, P.*; *Payongrik. L.* E. climber of the M and U. H. F. from 4,000 to 7,000 ft. Very common round Darjeeling. Fl. 12, fr. 9-10.

CHORIPETALUM UNDULATUM, A. DC. *Amilpati, P.* E. big climber of the M. H. F. from 3,000 to 6,000 ft. Fl. ?, fr. 12. Wood yellowish white, hard, with fine medullary rays.

ARDISIA HUMILIS, Vahl. Shrub of the L. H. F. undergrowth. Not common. Fl. 6-7, fr. 11·12.

ARDISIA FLORIBUNDA, Wall. Large shrub of the L. and M. H. F. up to 4,000 ft. Flowers pink, handsome.

ARDISIA CRENULATA, Vent. *Chumlani, P.*; *Denyok, L.* E. $\frac{2\text{-}6}{1\text{-}3+0\text{-}\frac{1}{2}}$. Small, low, single-stemmed shrub of the M. and U. H. F. undergrowth, from 4,000 to 8,000 ft. Fl. 5-6., fr. 11-12. Very pretty, either with its wax-like flowers in spring or brilliant red berries in winter.

ARDISIA INVOLUCRATA, Kurz. *Chumlani, P.*; *Denyok, L.* E. $\frac{5\text{-}10}{0\text{-}5+\frac{1}{2}\text{-}}$ of the M. P. F. *w.* and banks of streams in Terai and L. H. F. up to 1,000 ft. Fl. 6-7, fr. 1-2. Very pretty shrub.

ARDISIA MACROCARPA, Wall. Large shrub of the M. H. F. about 6,000 ft. Fr. 5.

SAPOTACEÆ.

SIDEROXYLON ARBOREUM, Ham. *Pahar Lampati, P.*; *Kulyatzo-kúng, L.* E. big tree of the L. and M. H. F. up to 4,000 ft. Fr. 6. Wood hard, heavy; used to make canoes. Leaves given to cattle.

SIDEROXYLON (ATTENUATUM, DC.). *Kulyatzo-kúng, L.* E. big tree of the L. and M. H. F. up to 4,000 ft. Fr. 10.

BASSIA BUTYRACEA, Roxb. *Choori, P.*; *Yel-kúng, L.* E. $\frac{40\text{-}50}{15\text{-}25+4\text{-}6}$. Big tree of the L. H. F. up to 4,000 ft. Fl. 12-1, fr. 5-6. Seeds eaten by Paharias and Lepchas. Wood good, but the tree generally grows very crooked.

NOTE.—Of *Ebenaceæ* I have never met with any species, but Hooker (Him. Journal) mentions *Diospyros Embryopteris*, Persoon, as growing in the Tista valley.

STYRACACEÆ.

SYMPLOCOS RACEMOSA, Roxb. *Chumlani, P.*; *Palyok-kúng, L.*; *Kaiday, M.*; *Singyen, Bh.* E. $\frac{15\text{-}20}{5\text{-}10+1\text{-}2}$ of the S. F., Sv. F., M. P. F. *d.* of Terai, and occasionally up to 7,000 ft. Fl. 11-12, fr. 5-6. Leaves give a mordant used with the Manjit dye.

SYMPLOCOS CAUDATA, Wall. *Oulia Kharani, P.* E. $\frac{10\text{-}15}{0\text{-}5+1\text{-}2}$ of the M. P. F. *w.* and L. H. F. Fl. 1-2.

SYMPLOCOS GLOMERATA, King. *Sanu Hingo, P.* E. $\frac{15\text{-}20}{5\text{-}10+1\text{-}2}$ of the M. P. F. and banks of streams in Terai and up to 6,000 ft. occasionally. Fl. 3, fr. 7. Wood strong.

SYMPLOCOS SPICATA, Roxb. *Palyok-kúng, L.* E. $\frac{20\text{-}30}{5\text{-}10+1\text{-}3}$ of the M. P. F. *w.* in Terai and up to 5,000 ft. Fl. 1-2. Leaves used in dyeing.

SYMPLOCOS POLYSTACHYA, Wall. Small tree of the M. H. F. about 5,000 ft. Fr. 8.

SYMPLOCOS RAMOSISSIMA, Wall. *Kala Kharani, L.*; *Tung-chong-kúng, L.* E. $\frac{15\text{-}20}{5\text{-}10+2\text{-}3}$ of the M. and U. H. F. from 5,000 to 7,000 ft. Fl. 5, fr. 10.

SYMPLOCOS LUCIDA, Wall. *Kharani, P.*; *Chashing, Bh.* E. $\frac{20\text{-}50}{10\text{-}20+3\text{-}4}$ of the U. H. F. from 6,000 to 10,000 ft. Very common about Darjeeling and on Tongloo. Wood white, soft, not used. Fl. 10.

SYMPLOCOS SP. *Lal Chandan, P.*; *Chandan, L.* E. $\frac{15\text{-}20}{5\text{-}10+2\text{-}3}$ of the U. H. F. Only seen by me on Thosum La, 8,000 ft. beyond Dumsong, and on Tongloo. Wood grey, with streaks of red; hard, close-grained. The red part, which is darkest in the root, is ground into a paste by Paharias and used in their religious ceremonies and for caste-marks. Fr. 10.

STYRAX SERRULATUM, Roxb. *Chamo-kúng, L.* E. $\frac{15\text{-}20}{5\text{-}10+1\text{-}2}$ of the Terai, L. and M. H. F., up to 6,000 ft. Fl. 3, fr. 7. Wood rather soft, but not liable to warp or split; used by Bhutias for prayer poles.

STYRAX SP. *Chamo-kúng, L.* E. small tree of the U. H. F. with much larger flowers and fruit than the preceding. Not uncommon round Darjeeling. Fl. 5, fr. 8.

OLEACEÆ.

OLEA DIOICA, Roxb. *Kala kiamoni, P.*; *Timbernyok, L.* L. tree of the M. P. F. *w.* in Terai and L. H. F. Not common. Fl. 4

OSMANTHUS FRAGRANS, Lour. *Tungrung-kúng, L.* E. $\frac{15\text{-}20}{5\text{-}10+1\text{-}2}$. Small tree of U. H. F. found about Darjeeling. Fl. 8, flowers very sweet-scented, with the scent of apricots.

LIGUSTRUM (ROBUSTUM, Hk. f. and T.). *Jamu, P.* Small tree of the L. H. F., only once met with. Fl. 8.

JASMINUM GRANDIFLORUM, Linn. Large shrub of about 7,000 ft., not common and perhaps escaped from cultivation. Fl. 5. Flowers yellow, scented.

JASMINUM DISPERMUM, Wall. *Irbo-lara, P.* Climbing shrub of U. H. about 6,000 to 7,000 ft. Common in Darjeeling. Flowers pink-white or lilac, very sweet-scented. Fl. 5, fr. 12.

JASMINUM LAURIFOLIUM, Roxb. Climbing shrub, common in L. and M. Hills, up to 6,000 ft. Flowers long-tubed, white, sweet-scented. Fl. 6.

JASMINUM PUBESCENS, Linn. *Parirajhar, P.* Small much-branched shrub of the Terai and L. H. F. up to 3,000 ft. Fl. 9, white, scented.

NOTE.—There are several other species of *Jasminum* besides, but too small to deserve mention. The lilac, *Syringa vulgaris*, Linn, has lately been introduced into Darjeeling Gardens, and the Naini Tal ash, *Fraxinus floribunda*, Wall., is being grown at Rungbool.

APOCYNEÆ.

ALSTONIA SCHOLARIS, R. Br. *Chatwan, Bg.*; *Chatiwan, P.*; *Purbo-kúng, L.* E. $\frac{40\text{-}60}{20\text{-}30+4\text{-}6}$ of the S. F. and M. P. F. *d.* of the Terai and L. H. F. up to 3,000 ft. Fl. 11, fr. 1. A fine handsome tree, with branches and leaves in whorls. Wood white, soft, even-grained; has been used for tea-boxes, but the tree is not sufficiently common to be much used.

ALSTONIA VENENATA, R. Br. *Chatwa, P.*; *Purbo-kúng, L.* Large shrub (?) of the L. H. F.; only once seen.

TABERNÆMONTANA CORONARIA, Willd. *Asuru, P.*; *Krim-kúng, L.* E. $\frac{6\text{-}10}{0\text{-}3+\frac{1}{2}\text{-}1}$ of the M. P. F. *w.* in Terai and L. H. F. up to 2,000 ft. Wood yellowish white, rather soft, close-grained, polishes well. Bark silvery-grey with whitish big lenticels. Often cultivated also in gardens in the Terai and Lower Hills.

PLUMERIA ACUTIFOLIA, Poiret. L. $\frac{15\text{-}20}{0\text{-}5+1\text{-}2}$. Small tree, cultivated in gardens in the Terai. Fine specimens may be seen on the old road at Mattigarha. Fl. 12.

OPHIOXYLON SERPENTINUM, Willd. Small under-shrub of up to 2 ft. high. Common in Terai and L. Hills up to 2,000 ft. Fl. fr. 4-8.

HOLARRHENA ANTIDYSENTERICA, Wall. *Kirra, P.* (?); *Karingi, P.*; *Dudhali, M.* L. $\frac{30\text{-}40}{10\text{-}20+2\text{-}3}$ of the S. F., Sv. F., M. P. F. *d.* of Terai and L. H. F. up to 3,000 ft. Fl. 5, fr. 8-9. Wood white, soft, shining. (There are two varieties, *glabra* and *pubescens.*)

HOLARRHENA SP. *Asari, P.* Small tree of the L. H. F. up to 4,000 ft., with bright scarlet flowers and bluish tinged leaves. Fl. 5, fr. 6-7.

WRIGHTIA TOMENTOSA, Röm and Sch. *Kæringi, P.*; *Selemnyok, L.* L. $\frac{20\text{-}40}{10\text{-}20+2\text{-}3}$ of the M. P. F. *d.* and L. H. F. up to 3,000 ft. Fl. 5-6, fr. 12-1. Wood yellowish white; said to be good, but small.

ICHNOCARPUS FRAGRANS, Wall. *Doari-lara, P.*; *Yokchoun-rik, L.* Large climber of the M. and U. H. F. from 4,000 to 7,000 ft. Fl. 6. Gives an Indian rubber-like milk.

NOTE.—There are three other species, as well as two of the section *Aganosma*, which I omit, as I have not the correct specific names. They are all climbers, found at about 1,000 to 6,000 ft.

CHONEMORPHA MACROPHYLLA, G. Don. *Yokchoun-rik, L.* Large climber of the M. H. F. from 4,000 to 6,000 ft. Fl. 5-6, fr. 1-2. Gives a good sort of caoutchouc. Flowers very handsome, often covering the tops of tall trees with a sheet of white.

BEAUMONTIA GRANDIFLORA, Wall. *Barbari, P.* Large climber of the M. P. F. *w.* in Terai, L. and M. H. F. up to 5,000 ft. Bark corky, thick. Flowers big, trumpet-shaped, very handsome. Fl. 2-3.

NOTE.—Besides *Plumeria* a few other species are cultivated in gardens in the Terai and Lower Hills, such as *Nerium oleander*, L.; *Allamanda cathartica*, L.; *Thevetia neriifolia*, Juss.

ASCLEPIADACEÆ.

PERIPLOCA CALOPHYLLA, Falc. *Mas-lara, P.*; *Purgeen-rik, L.* Small, pretty, glabrous shrub of the M. and U. H. F. from 3,000 to 6,000 ft. Fl. 3, fr. 7.

CALOTROPIS GIGANTEA, R. Br. *Madar, H.*; *Auk, P.* Shrub, not uncommon in the Terai forests. Fl. 5.

RAPHISTEMMA PULCHELLUM, Wall. *Chongfibrik, L.* Handsome flowered small climber of the L. H. F. Fl. 8.

GYMNEMA TINGENS, W. and A. Climbing shrub of L. H. F. Fl. 5.

PERGULARIA ODORATISSIMA, Linn. *Simpletbuk, L.* Large climbing shrub of Terai. Fl. 5. Roots eaten by Lepchas.

MARSDENIA TINCTORIA, R. Br. *Kali-lara, P.*; *Ryôm, L.* Climbing shrub of L. H. F. (I have never seen this, but have little doubt that it is the *Ryôm* of the Lepchas, used to give a black or bluish black dye.)

NOTE.—There are many other species, chiefly small climbers.

LOGANIACEÆ.

BUDDLEIA ASIATICA, Lour. *Newarpati, . P*; *Pondam-kúng, L.* E. $\frac{10\text{-}15}{0\text{-}3+\frac{1}{2}\text{-}\frac{3}{4}}$ of the Sv. F. and old cultivations in the Terai and L. H. F. up to 5,000 ft. Fl. 12-1. Exceedingly common in old cultivated land, both in Terai and Hills. Very pretty with its long spikes of sweet-scented white flowers.

BUDDLEIA PANICULATA, Wall. *Bejunpati, P.* E. big shrub, rather rare, of about 6,000 ft. altitude. Fl. 3-4.

BUDDLEIA COLVILLEI. *Pyashing, Bh.* $\frac{E}{L}$ (?) $\frac{15\text{-}20}{5\text{-}10+1\text{-}2}$ of the R. F. about 10,000 ft. Common on Tongloo. Fl. 8, fr. 11. Very handsome with its dark masses of crimson flowers. Wood reddish brown, with fine medullary rays and well-marked small annual rings.

FAGRŒA OBOVATA, Wall. *Suna-khari, P.* E. tree or epiphytic tree of the L. H. F. Only once found by me, and that on the Bhutan frontier in the Jaldoka valley. Fr. 3.

GARDNERIA OVATA, Wall. *Takpadik, L.* Climber, not common; found at about 7,000 to 8,000 ft. Fl. 8.

BORAGINEÆ.

CORDIA MYXA, Linn. *Bohari, Bg.*; *Boeri, P.*; *Nimat-kúng, L.* L. $\frac{20\text{-}40}{10\text{-}20+2\text{-}6}$ of the K. S. F. and M. P. F. *d.* in Terai and L. H. F. Also in Lower Terai, isolated in thickets or along streams. Fl. 3, fr. 6. Wood greyish brown, light, soft but durable; used for canoes. Fruit occasionally eaten.

CORDIA GRANDIS, Roxb. *Asari, P.* L. $\frac{20\text{-}30}{10\text{-}15+2\text{-}3}$ on the banks of streams in Terai and L. Hills, especially west of the Balasan. Fl. 9-10, fr. 1.

EHRETIA SERRATA, Roxb. *Chillay, P.* E. $\frac{15\text{-}20}{5\text{-}10+1\text{-}2}$ of the L. H. F. Fl. 3, fr. 6.

EHRETIA (LŒVIS, Roxb.) *Boeri, P.* L. $\frac{40\text{-}60}{20\text{-}30+4\text{-}5}$ of the M. and U. H. F. from 4,000 to 7,000 ft. Fl. ?, fr. 10. Very common in old cultivated lands in some places, as on the small spur next to, and west of, the old Pashok Gumpa, forming almost pure young forest. Wood yellowish white, rough, hard; used occasionally for building, more often for charcoal. The leaves of young trees are often 9-12 in. long by 6 in. broad.

EHRETIA WALLICHIANA, Hk. f. and T. *Dowari, P.*; *Kalet-kúng, L.* Small tree of the L. and M. H. F. from 2,000 to 6,000 ft. Fl. 5, fr. 6-7. Resembles the next above, but has much smaller leaves, and is found lower down.

TOURNEFORTIA VIRIDIFLORA, Wall. *Ampati-lara, P.*; *Tungrongrik, L.* Climber of the Terai and L. H. F. Fl. fr. at most seasons. Wood dark-brown, soft.

CONVOLVULACEÆ.

RIVEA ORNATA, Choisy. Climbing shrub of S. F. in the Terai. Commoner in the southern forests and in the meadow land between the Jhars. Fl. 7-8, fr. 12. Seeds eaten.

ARGYREIA (SPECIOSA, Sweet). *Kuntun-rik, L.* Large climber of the L. H. F. and valleys. Leaves with dense white tomentum beneath. Fl. 10.

ARGYREIA CAPITATA, Choisy. *Dangeen-rik, L.* Climber of the M. P. F. *d.*, banks of streams and waste places in the Terai, also L. H. F. Fl. 10-11.

ARGYREIA SETOSA, Choisy. Climber in similar places to above. Fl. 10.

ARGYREIA (POMACEA, Choisy). *Bairi-lara, P.* Common climber of banks of streams in K. S. F., S. F. and M. P. F. *d.* in Terai and L. H. F. Berry bright yellow, ripe 1.

IPOMŒA ATROPURPUREA, Wall. Climber of Terai and L. H. F.

PORANA VOLUBILIS, Burm. *Papray-lara, P.*; *Mom-rik, L.* Climber of the L. H. F. up to 5,000 ft. Fl. 10-11. Leaves smooth, thin.

PORANA PANICULATA, Roxb. *Badulpati, P.*; *Kadiwan-rik, L.* Climber of the L. H. F. up to 3,000 ft. Fl. 11-12. Leaves white, tomentose. These two species both climb over tall trees, covering them in the flowering season with a sheet of white.

NOTE.—There are many other species, especially of *Argyreia*, which might be mentioned if they were properly determined. *Porana grandiflora* is a showy crimson-flowered climber of the neighbourhood of Darjeeling, flowering in August; and *Ipomœa* (*Quamoclit*) *coccinea* may be seen covering the trees and bushes in the Lower Hills with its brilliant scarlet flowers in November mixed with the white masses of *Porana volubilis* and *paniculata*, but the real home of *Convolvulaceæ* is in the tangled thickets and waste places near rivers in the Terai, and especially between the Chel and the Murti.

SOLANEÆ.

SOLANUM VERBASCIFOLIUM, Linn. *Dursul, P.*; *Sivor-kúng, L.* E. $\frac{10\text{-}20}{5\text{-}10+\frac{1}{2}\text{-}1\frac{1}{2}}$ of the L. H. F. and valleys of inner hills; also occasionally met with in the Terai, chiefly in waste places. Fl. 9, fr. 11-12.

SOLANUM INDICUM, Willd. *Bhi, P.* Large branching thorny shrub; very common in waste places, old village sites, &c., in Terai. Fl. fr. 12-2.

NOTE.—*Solanum crassipetalum* and *Solanum membranaceum* are small shrubs not uncommon in the M. and U. H. F. from 4,000 to 7,000 ft., and the common chili is often found growing into a shrub 6-10 ft. high in old cultivations and on the sites of old villages.

SCROPHULARINEÆ.

WIGHTIA GIGANTEA, Wall. *Lakori, P.*; *Bop-kúng, L.* L. huge epiphytic tree, often far overtopping other big trees. Often found as a tree on its own roots 60 ft. high and 3-4 ft. girth. Fl. 10. Its stem sends out horizontal stem-clasping roots. M. and U. H. F. from 3,000 to 7,000 ft. Wood soft, but does not warp; used by the Lamas to make idols for their temples.

GESNERACEÆ.

LEPTOBŒA MULTIFLORA, Bth. *Tungrangmook, L.* Small shrub of the L. H. F., common about Pankabari. Fl. 8.

BIGNONIACEÆ.

STEREOSPERMUM CHELONOIDES, DC. *Parari, P.*; *Singyen-kúng, L.* L. $\frac{40\text{-}60}{20\text{-}30+4\text{-}6}$. Common tree in the S. F. and M. P. F. *d.* of the Terai and in the L. H. F. up to 2,000 ft. Fl. 4, fr. 11. Wood greyish white, with very numerous narrow medullary rays, and pores of different sizes, arranged in wavy lines. Used by Paharias for house-building and all purposes, but not yet much sought for in the district. Would probably be good for tea-boxes. Fruit long, curved, angled, smooth. Leaves smooth. Flowers pink-brown, fragrant.

STEREOSPERMUM SUAVEOLENS, DC. *Parari, P.* (?); *Singyen-kúng.* L. $\frac{40\text{-}50}{15\text{-}20+4\text{-}6}$ of the S. F. and M. P. F. *d.* of the Terai and L. H. F. up to 2,000 ft. Fl. 4, fr. 11. Wood not known. Not so common as the former, from which it is easily recognized by the long straight, cylindrical, rough capsule, and rough leaves.

NOTE.—These two trees require further investigation. The flowers of No. 1 are certainly not yellow, as described in Brandis's *Forest Flora*, Kurz's *Preliminary Forest Report of Pegu*, and Roxburgh's *Flora Indica*. The wood also is described in the books mentioned as "orange-yellow," which it never is in the Darjeeling Terai.

CALOSANTHES INDICA, Bl. *Totilla, P.* L. $\frac{20\text{-}30}{10\text{-}20+1\text{-}3}$ of the S. F., Sv. F. and M. P. F. *d.* of Terai and L. H. F. up to 2,000 ft. Fl. 5-6, fr. 12-1. Bark brownish white, gives a green juice when cut. Wood white, light, even-grained, not used. Recognized by its large bi-pinnate leaves, terminal yellowish red racemes, and large flat sword-like fruit.

ACANTHACEÆ.

THUNBERGIA GRANDIFLORA, Roxb. *Chong-la fib-rik, L.* Large handsome climber of the Terai and L. H. F. Fl. 8.

THUNBERGIA COCCINEA, Wall. Large climber of the L. M. and U. H. F. from 2,000 to 7,000 ft. Fl. 8. Wood soft, fibrous. Stem grey-brown, rough, with swollen nodes.

NOTE.—*Thunbergia lutea*, T. And., is a pretty yellow-flowered, bulbous-rooted climber peculiar to Darjeeling, and *T. fragrans*, Roxb., a small white-flowered, scented climber of the undergrowth in the S. F. and L. H. F.

DŒDALACANTHUS SPLENDENS, T. And. *Shechin, P.* Small shrub 3-6 ft. high, of the undergrowth in the S. F. of the Terai and L. H. F. up to 2,000 ft. Fl. 12-1. Flowers pink.

DŒDALACANTHUS (NERVOSUS, T. And.). *Shechin, P.*; *Topatnyok, L.* Shrub 4-10 ft. of the M. P. F. *w.* of Terai and L. H. F. valleys. Fl. 12-1. Flowers deep blue.

BARLERIA CRISTATA, Roxb. A small showy shrub of the L. H. F. dry ridges among Sâl. Fl. 10-11. Often found cultivated in gardens as a bush 3-4 ft. high.

BARLERIA CŒRULEA, Roxb. A small pretty shrub of L. and M. Hills up to 4,000 ft. Fl. 11. Also occasionally found cultivated.

NOTE.—Of the genus *Strobilanthes* there are some eight to ten species, ranging throughout the whole district, from the moist forests of the Terai to the summit of Tongloo, 10,000 ft. Some few are shrubs, rising to 6 ft. or more in height, *e.g.* *Strobilanthes* with lilac flowers, and *S. pectinatus*, T. And., with blue flowers and thick hairy leaves. *S. maculatus*, Nees, is a pretty blue-flowered shrub with variegated leaves, of about 4,000 ft. *S. divaricatus*, T. And., with dark purple flowers, is very common in Darjeeling. *S. Wallichii*, Nees, and *S. pentstemonoides*, T. And., are found up to 10,000 ft., and *S. auriculatus*, Nees, is a pretty shrub of the undergrowth in the Sâl forests of the Tista and Great Rangít. *Æchmanthera Wallichii*, Nees, resembling *Strobilanthes*, is common in the Lower Hills and valleys up to 4,000 ft.

PHLOGACANTHUS THYRSIFLORUS, Nees. *Sua, P.*; *Shechin, P.*; *Sumcher-kúng, L.* E. $\frac{10\text{-}15}{0\text{-}3+\frac{1}{2}\text{-}1}$ of the M. P. F. *w.* and banks of streams in the Terai and L. H. F., especially damp places, up to 2,000 ft. Fl. 1-3. Wood white, hard, heavy, close-grained, with numerous very narrow medullary rays. Flowers flame colour, very handsome.

PHLOGACANTHUS PUBINERVIS, T. And. *Chunkyek-kúng, L.* Shrub of about 6 ft. high of L. and M. H. F. Fl. 1, rather rare.

ADHATODA VASICA, Nees. Large shrub. Only once seen by me, and then probably planted. Fl. 3.

JUSTICIA GENDARUSSA, L. A small shrub of the damp forests of the Terai.

VERBENACEÆ.

CALLICARPA ARBOREA, Roxb. *Goehlo, P.*; *Jamti, M.*; *Sung-a-kúng, L.* E. $\frac{20\text{-}40}{5\text{-}20+2\text{-}4}$ of the S. F., Sv. F., M. P. F. *d.* of the Terai and L. H. F. up to 3,000 ft. Very common in old Mechi or Lepcha cultivations. Fl. 4, fr. 11. Almost universal in the Terai, but most common in dry mixed forests of small trees on good soil and in Savannahs. Bark grey-brown. Wood brownish white, of good grain, tolerably heavy; only used for charcoal.

CALLICARPA LANATA, Linn. *Sung-a-kúng, L.* E. $\frac{20\text{-}30}{5\text{-}15+2\text{-}3}$ of the L. and M. H. F. from 1,000 to 6,000 ft., chiefly and almost entirely in old cultivations. Fl. 7. Distinguished from the first by its leaves having soft white tomentum, while those of *C. arborea* have only a slight short stellate tomentum.

CALLICARPA RUBELLA, Ldl. *Sugroo-mook, L.* Large shrub or small tree of the L. and M. H. F. about 3,000 ft. Fl. 6, fr. 10.

CALLICARPA CANA, Linn. Common shrub along roadsides and in waste places in the Lower Terai. Fl. 8, fr. 10.

TECTONA GRANDIS, L. fil., is not indigenous to the district, but is being planted experimentally at Bamunpokri. The plantation was commenced in 1868, and the trees then planted are now 20-25 ft. in height, with a girth of 1-2 ft. A small experimental plantation was also once formed at Mohurgong, and others have been made in the Julpigori Division, at Ramshai Hât and Fallacotta, but none of these have succeeded. It has been tried in the cinchona plantations in the Tista valley, but without success. A few plants grown at the forester's house at Panigatta, west of the Balasan, have however grown very well.

PREMNA INTEGRIFOLIA, Linn. *Gineri, P.* L. $\frac{20\text{-}30}{10\text{-}15+3\text{-}4}$ of the M. P. F. *d.* of the Terai. The leaves when bruised have an unpleasant smell. Stem often thorny. Bark grey-white. Wood white, tinted green from the sap when freshly cut, hard, close-grained.

PREMNA LATIFOLIA, Roxb. *Gineri, P.*; *Michapgong, L.* L. $\frac{20\text{-}30}{10\text{-}15+3\text{-}5}$ of the K. S. F. and M. P. F. *d.* in Terai and L. H. F. up to 2,000 ft. Fl. 7. Bark grey white. Wood white or greenish white, hard, heavy, close-grained, with numerous very narrow fine medullary rays; a good kind for rubbing to obtain fire.

PREMNA BARBATA, Wall. *Michapnok, L.* Small tree of the S. F. and M. P. F. *d.* in Terai and L. H. F. up to 2,000 ft. Wood hard, used to obtain fire. Fl. 4.

PREMNA TOMENTOSA, Willd. *Gwyheli, P.*; *Sungna-kúng, L.* E. $\frac{30\text{-}50}{10\text{-}20+2\text{-}3}$ of the L. H. F. banks of rivers. Fl. 1-2, fr. 6. Bark white, thin; stem very irregularly indented. Wood yellowish white, hard, close-grained, medullary rays very numerous and fine.

PREMNA MUCRONATA, Roxb. *Kala bogoti, P.* Small tree of the L. H. F. up to 3,000 ft. Fr. 6.

PREMNA SCANDENS, Roxb. *Sindri-lara, P.*; *Monkakrig, L.* Large climbing shrub, very common on the banks of streams in M. P. F. *w.* and in the Lower Terai, making a dense close network of straggling branches.

PREMNA INTERRUPTA, Wall. Large climbing shrub of the U. H. F. from 5,000 to 8,000 ft. Fl. 5-7.

PREMNA RACEMOSA, Wall. Large climbing shrub of the L. and M. H. F. from 2,000 to 5,000 ft. Fl. 5-6.

PREMNA HERBACEA, Roxb., is a small herbaceous plant from a perennial root-stock, coming up after the jungle fires in S. F. and Sv. F. in the Terai, and covering the ground with its rosette-like leaves and small yellow flowers.

GMELINA ARBOREA, Roxb. *Gambari, P.*; *Numbor-kúng, L.* E. $\frac{40\text{-}60}{15\text{-}25+4\text{-}8}$ of the K. S. F. and M. P. F. *d.* in Terai and L. H. F. up to 3,000 ft. Fl. 3. Bark grey or brownish white, exfoliating in small scales. Stem rather irregular, but cylindrical. Wood yellowish white, strong, light, with numerous very fine medullary rays and pores of different sizes, chiefly large. Is very easily worked, and does not warp; is little used, however, in spite of its being one of the best of the Lower Hill woods. The leaves are much lopped to feed cattle.

VITEX HETEROPHYLLA, Roxb. *Neri, P.*; *Murkut-kúng, L.* E. $\frac{30\text{-}50}{15\text{-}20+3\text{-}5}$ of the L. H. F. up to 4,000 ft. Fl. 7. Wood said to be very good.

VITEX ALTISSIMA, Linn. Tree only found in the southern Sâl forests, such as the Tookria, Sath Bhaia and Tehsilpur Jhars.

VITEX TRIFOLIA, Linn. *Pajpati, P.* Small tree, only found cultivated in the Terai. Used to make hedges. Big specimens may be seen at Mattigarha, on the old road.

CLERODENDON SERRATUM, Spreng. *Chue, P.*; *Yi-kúng, L.* Large shrub of the S. F., Sv. F. and M. P. F. *d.* of Terai and L. H. F. up to 3,000 ft. Fl. 3-8, light blue.

CLERODENDRON INFORTUNATUM, Linn. *Chitu, P.; Kadungnyok, L.* Large shrub of waste places and old village sites in the Terai; occasionally, but rarely, in forest. Fl. 1-3, white tinged with pink.

CLERODENDRON SIPHONANTHUS, R. Br. Tall straight-stemmed shrub of S. F., Sv. F. and M. P. F. *d.* in Terai and L. H. F. up to 2,000 ft. Recognized by its long-tubed white corolla, blue berries, red calyx, and long narrow leaves.

. CLERODENDRON DENTATUM, Roxb. *Chitu, P.; Rotdhip, L.* Handsome shrub of L. H. F. damp places up to 3,000 ft. Fl. 6-7, bright scarlet.

NOTE.—I am not quite sure of the name of this, or if it is not *C. urticæfolium*, Roxb., but both are probably found. Both Lepchas and Paharias are very fond of the flowers, wearing them in their pugrees.

CLERODENDRON GRATUM, Wall. Straggling shrub of the M. H. F. about 4,000 to 5,000 ft. Fl. 10-11.

CLERODENDRON BRACTEATUM, Wall. *Chitu, P.; Kadungnyok, L.* Large shrub or small tree of the L. and M. H. F. from 2,500 to 4,000 ft., chiefly in old cultivations. Fl. 6, fr. 8.

CLERODENDRON COLEBROOKIANUM, Walp. *Kadungbi, L.* E. $\frac{15\text{-}20}{0\text{-}10+1\text{-}2}$ of the M. H. F. chiefly second-growth forest, and very common from 3,000 to 6,000 ft. Fl. 8-10, fr. 12. Bark silvery grey. Wood pink-white with bands of yellow, soft, with fine medullary rays and large pores arranged in nearly concentric lines. The whole plant has a strong disagreeable smell. The flowers are white and berries bright turquoise blue. The young leaves are eaten by Lepchas.

CLERODENDRON NUTANS, Wall. *Baichua, P.; Tongsor-kúng, L.* Shrub of the L. and M. H. F. damp places, from the plains up to 5,000 ft. Fl. 9, fr. 1.

HOLMSKIOLDIA SANGUINEA, Retz. *Sarputtia, P.; Sivettachim, L.* Large climbing shrub of Terai, chiefly banks of streams and L. H. F. up to 2,000 ft. Fl. 12-1, very handsome, with scarlet calyx and corolla.

. CARYOPTERIS WALLICHIANA, Schauer. *Shechin, P.; Matet-kúng, L.* Large shrub of the L. H. F. dry aspects up to 2,000 ft. Fl. 12-1, lilac-blue. Bark papery, peeling off in vertical strips. Wood grey-brown, hard, with the scent of cherry wood.

LABIATÆ.

TEUCRIUM MACROSTACHYUM, Wall. *Gurupis, P.; Chúng-kúng, L.* E. $\frac{20\text{-}30}{0\text{-}10+1\text{-}3}$. Very common in all old cultivations, graziers' resting-places and cleared spots in the U. H. F. from 5,000 to 8,000 ft. Fl. 2. Has long upright spikes of yellow-white flowers with long stamens, somewhat resembling a "bottle brush" when rather old. A quantity of sweet juice exudes from the flowers, and this is sucked by Paharia herdsmen. Bark yellow-brown, corky. Wood yellowish white, hard, close-grained, with very fine narrow medullary rays but warping very badly; very quick growing. C. B. Clarke, in Linnean Society's Journal, 1876, calls this *Colquhounia sp.*

COLEBROOKIA OPPOSITIFOLIA, Sm. *Dosúl, P.* Large shrub of the Sâl forests of the Tista and Rangít valleys; occasionally on the outer hills. Fl. 1-2. The down is used by Paharias to extract worms from bad sores on their legs.

AMARANTACEÆ.

DEERINGIA BACCATA, Moq. Climber of the K. S. F. and waste places in the Terai and L. H. F. up to 4,000 ft. Fl. 8, fr. 1. Fruit a red berry.

AERVA SCANDENS, Wall. Large climber of the M. and U. H. F. from 5,000 to 7,000 ft. Fl. 9-10. Covers even tall trees with its masses of handsome flowers and soft whitish leaves.

POLYGONACEÆ.

POLYGONUM MOLLE, Don. *Totnye, P.* Large trailing shrub, very common all over the Darjeeling Hills, sending its branches even over big trees. The stems grow to about 1 ft. in girth, the shoots are eaten by Paharias and Lepchas, and resemble rhubarb in flavour. Fl. 6-7, fr. 11-12. Wood white, with many medullary rays and much pith. Stem knotty.

POLYGONUM CRISPATUM, Ham. A handsome shrub of the higher ranges about 10,000 ft. Fl. fr. 10-11.

LAURACEÆ.

CINNAMOMUM TAMALA, Nees. *Singoli, P.*; *Nupsorg-kúng, L.* E. $\frac{30\text{-}40}{10\text{-}20 + 3\text{-}4}$ of M. P. F. *w.* in Terai and L. H. F. damp localities. Fl. 3-4, fr. 7-8. Common in the forests of the valleys of the Mahanadi and Tista, but not much found west of the Mahanadi. Bark brown with white specks, aromatic, largely exported to Lower Bengal under the name of "taj." The tree coppices well and could be made profitable, as the damp forests in which it grows are not generally rich in first class timber. The leaves also are aromatic, and are collected, dried, and sold in the bazaars by the name of "tespat."

CINNAMOMUM OBTUSIFOLIUM, Nees. *Singoli, P.*; *Nupsor-kúng, L.* E. $\frac{50\text{-}60}{20\text{-}30 + 4\text{-}5}$ of the M. P. F. *w.* in Terai, L. H. F. and M. H. F. up to 7,000 ft. Bark and leaves aromatic, like the preceding, but not so much used.

CINNAMOMUM CAUDATUM. *Kharsoni, P.*; *Sanging-kúng, L.* E. $\frac{40\text{-}50}{10\text{-}20 + 4\text{-}6}$ of the L. and M. H. F from 1,000 to 5,000 ft. Fl. 8, fr. 11.

CINNAMOMUM GLANDULIFERUM, Meissn. *Malligiri, P.*; *Rohu-kúng, L.*; *Gunserai, M.* E. $\frac{40\text{-}60}{20\text{-}30+6\text{-}10}$ of the M. P. F. *w.* in Terai and in L. H. F. up to 4,000 ft. Not now common, but has probably been so and been formerly cut out. Bark and wood highly scented. Wood yellowish brown, open-grained, soft, easily worked and durable, very good for furniture and boxes, especially for clothes, as it keeps off insects.

CINNAMOMUM IMPRESSINERVIUM, Meissn. Large tree of the M. H. F. from 4,000 to 6,000 ft. Not common.

PHŒBE LANCEOLATA, Nees. E. $\frac{30\text{-}40}{15\text{-}20+3\text{-}4}$ of the M. P. F. *w.* in Terai and L. H. F. up to 3,000 ft. Also, but rather different in appearance, M. and U. H. F. up to 6,000 ft. Fl. 4, fr. 10. Wood of the Lower Hill variety yellowish brown, hard, close-grained, easily worked.

PHŒBE GLAUCESCENS, Nees. *Surool, P.* E. $\frac{20\text{-}30}{10\text{-}20+3\text{-}4}$ of the L. H. F. up to 3,000 ft. Not common. Fl. 2-3, fr. 3.

PHŒBE ATTENUATA, Nees. *Dudri, P.*; *Lepchaphal, P.* (local); *Phani-kúng, L.* E. $\frac{80\text{-}100}{30\text{-}40+8\text{-}12}$ of the M. and U. H. F. from 4,000 to 8,000 ft., smaller at higher elevations; very common about 5,000 to 6,000 ft. Fl. 5, fr. 10-11. A very fine large handsome tree. Wood yellowish grey, with bands of a darker colour, light, open-grained but durable, and much used for building purposes. Fruit large: when ripe, the size of a walnut. Eaten eagerly by Lepchas, whence the name "Lepchaphal," which appears to be only local, given by the Paharias in and about Darjeeling. This is the *Actinodaphne sp.* mentioned by C. B. Clarke in the Linnean Society's Journal, 1876.

MACHILUS ODORATISSIMUS, Nees. *Kawala, P.*; *Lali, P.*; *Jagrikat, P.*; *Phàmlet-kúng, L.* $\frac{E}{L}$ (?) $\frac{80\text{-}100}{30\text{-}40+8\text{-}12}$ of the M. P. F. of Terai, L. M. and U. H. F. up to 8,000 ft. Fl. 5, fr. 10. Very variable in size and shape of leaf; the darker longer leaved kind being generally called *Lali*, the smaller leaved one *Kawala* or *Kawlo* in the plains. Wood generally red, rather light, open-grained, but durable; often lighter coloured, with bands of yellowish-brown or grey. Much used for building native houses; not liable to warp.

BEILSCHMIEDIA ROXBURGHIANA, Nees. *Kanyoo-kúng, L.* Small tree of the L. and M. H. F. about 2,000 to 5,000 ft. Fl. fr. 6. Fruit black, with a bloom on it like a plum.

NOTE.—*Tarsing, P.*, somewhat resembles this, but I have never found the flowers or fruit, though it is very common. The wood is now much used for tea-boxes, for temporary houses, etc.

CRYPTOCARYA FLORIBUNDA, Nees. E. $\frac{40\text{-}50}{10\text{-}20+3\text{-}4}$ of the L. and M. H. F. up to 4,000 ft. Fl. fr. 4.

CRYPTOCARYA AMYGDALINA, Nees. *Patmero, P.*; *Kaledzo, L.* E. $\frac{30\text{-}40}{10\text{-}20+3\text{-}4}$ of the L. H. F. up to 3,000 ft. Fl. 2, fr. 8. Fruit black.

TETRANTHERA LAURIFOLIA, Jacq. *Suppatnyok, L.* E. tree of L. H. F. up to 3,000 ft. Fl. 8.

TETRANTHERA AMARA, Nees. *Likh Paieli, P.; Safednyok, L.* E. small tree of U. H. F. about 6,000 ft. Fl. 10.

TETRANTHERA SALICIFOLIA. *Paieli, P.* E. small tree of Terai M. P. F. *w.*, especially in damp places and near the banks of streams. Fl. 3.

TETRANTHERA TOMENTOSA, Roxb. *Phusri, P.; Phane-kúng, L.* E. $\frac{50\text{-}70}{20\text{-}30+4\text{-}6}$ of the U. H. F. from 6,000 to 8,000 ft. Fl. 10-11. Wood yellowish white; not much used.

TETRANTHERA SERICEA, Wall. E. small tree of U. H. F. and up to 10,000 ft. Fl. fr. 11.

TETRANTHERA POLYANTHA, Wall. *Siltimber, P.; Terhilsok-kúng, L.* E. $\frac{30\text{-}40}{15\text{-}20+2\text{-}3}$ of the M. H. F., especially in old cultivated land; from 3,000 to 6,000 ft. it is the commonest species. Bark green. Wood white, tough. Fl. 11-12, fr. 1-2.

TETRANTHERA GLAUCA, Wall. *Sempat, P.* E. small tree of M. P. F. *w.* in Terai and L. H. F. Fl. 3.

TETRANTHERA MONOPETALA, Roxb. *Ratmanti, P.; Kudmero, P.; Suphut-kúng, L.* E. $\frac{30\text{-}40}{15\text{-}20+4\text{-}5}$ of the M. P. F. *d.* and S. F. in Terai. Not uncommon in Savannahs. Fl. 3-4, fr. 6-7. Wood yellowish white; not used.

TETRANTHERA LÆTA, Wall. *Akhaterwa, P.; Phamlet-kúng, L.; Chimplet-kúng, L.* E. $\frac{20\text{-}30}{10\text{-}15+2\text{-}3}$ of the M. P. F. *w.* of Terai and L. H. F. Fl. 12-1, fr. 6—red-coloured.

ACTINODAPHNE OBOVATUM, Hk. f. and T. *Muslindi, P.; Pohor-kúng, L.* E. $\frac{60\text{-}80}{20\text{-}30+4\text{-}5}$ of the M. P. F. *w.* in Terai and L. H. F. valleys up to 2,000 ft. Very handsome with its large often whorled leaves, often 12 to 18 inches long and white underneath, and softly pubescent leaf buds. (? *Litsæa lanuginosa*, Nees, of Brandis's *Forest Flora.*)

LITSÆA CONSIMILIS, Nees. *Pooteli, P.* E. $\frac{20\text{-}30}{10\text{-}15+2\text{-}3}$ of the M. and U. H. F. from 4,000 to 8,000 ft. Fl. 2. Wood yellow, close-grained, hard, but light; when planed has a bright lustre, as if polished.

DAPHNIDIUM PULCHERRIMUM, Nees. *Sisi, P.; Nupsor-kúng, L.* E. $\frac{60\text{-}80}{20\text{-}30+4\text{-}5}$ of the U. H. F. from 6,000 to 8,000 ft. Fl. 5, fr. 9-10. Wood white, soft, but does not warp easily; used for building, to make cattle yokes, &c.

DAPHNIDIUM ELONGATUM, Nees. *Pooalay, P.; Phusri, P.; Paieli, P.; Phamlet, L.* E. $\frac{40\text{-}60}{20\text{-}30+4\text{-}5}$ of the U. H. F. from 6,000 to 8,000 ft. Fl. 9-10, fr. 5-6. Wood light yellow, soft, light, easily worked, used for building.

APERULA NEESIANA, Bl. *Kirima, P.; Tirhilsok-kúng, L.* E. $\frac{10\text{-}20}{5\text{-}10 + 1\text{-}2}$ of the U. H. F. from 6,000 to 10,000 ft. Fl. fr. 5-6. Very common about Senchul. Leaves and fruit very aromatic, lemon-scented; the fruit is eaten by Lepchas.

PROTEACEÆ.

Helicia Cochin-Chinensis, Lour. E. $\frac{20\text{-}30}{10\text{-}15+2\text{-}3}$. Found beween 2,000 and 4,000 ft. Not common.

Helicia robusta, Wall. E. $\frac{20\text{-}30}{10\text{-}15+2\text{-}3}$ between 2,000 and 4,000 ft., chiefly in open ground or in coppice woods of chestnut and *Schima*. Wood pretty, pinkish white with very broad medullary rays; heavy, but not durable. Fl. 6-7, fr. 3-4.

LORANTHACEÆ.

Viscum (album, L.). *Hurchu, P.* Parasitic shrub. Not very common. Fl. fr. 12. Found in Darjeeling at 7,000 ft. on maple and other trees.

Viscum attenuatum, DC. *Hurchu, P.* Parasitic shrub. Common in the U. H. F. on many kinds of trees—maple, chestnut, &c. Fl. 12, fr. 5. I found this and the preceding growing together on a maple (*Acer Campbellii*) in Darjeeling in December 1875.

Loranthus farinosus, Desr. *Ajeru, P.* (name for all kinds). Parasitic shrub. Common in S. F. and M. P. F. in Terai, especially on sâl.

Loranthus pentapetalus, Roxb. Parasitic shrub. Common in M. and U. H. F. from 4,000 to 8,000 ft. on maple, oak, chestnut and other trees.

Loranthus (graciliflorus, Wall.). Parasitic shrub. Very pretty with its bright crimson flowers. In L. H. F. about 2,000 ft. Found on *Schima*, &c. Fl. 4-5.

Loranthus viridiflorus, Wall. Parasitic shrub, with banded flowers. M. P. F. and S. F. in Terai. Found chiefly on sâl and *Schima*. Fl. 4.

Loranthus longiflorus, Desr. *Proosti, L.* Large parasitic shrub, with long handsome scarlet flowers. Common in Terai forests on sâl, siris, and other trees, and in L. and M. H. F. up to 6,000 ft. Fl. 5-6.

Loranthus (globosus, Roxb.). Parasitic shrub. Very common on sâl in the Terai forests, especially Sivoke.

Loranthus pentandrus, Linn. Large parasitic shrub of about 4,000 to 6,000 ft. alt.

Note.—There are many other species, which, it is hoped, may be added hereafter.

SANTALACEÆ.

Pyrularia edulis, A. DC. *Sufhyi-kúng, L.* L. $\frac{20\text{-}30}{5\text{-}10+1\text{-}2}$ of hills from 3,000 to 6,000 ft. Fl. 3, fr. 7. Bark thin, greenish grey. Wood hard, white, with big medullary rays; used by Bhutias to make implements of butter-making. Fruit eaten by the Lepchas.

HENSLOWIA HETERANTHA, Hk. f. *Ajiru, P.* Large parasitical shrub, sometimes apparently on its own roots, of the M. and U. H. F. from 4,000 to 7,000 ft. Found on *Quercus, Eugenia,* &c. Fl. 3, fr. 7.

ELÆAGNACEÆ.

ELÆAGNUS LATIFOLIA, L. *Jarila, P.* Occasionally a small tree of about 2 ft. girth, but more generally a rambling thorny shrub. Common about 4,000 to 6,000 ft., but occasionally found on the banks of streams in the Terai. Fl. fr. 3. Fruit edible. Wood yellowish white, hard, with conspicuous medullary rays.

THYMELÆCEÆ.

EDGEWORTHIA GARDNERI, Meissn. *Aryili, P.*; *Kaghuti, P.* A large shrub. Not common in the Darjeeling district—indeed only once seen by me at Ging, just below the chapel. In Nepal it is exceedingly common, and is the principal plant used in the manufacture of paper, of which it furnishes the best and whitest description.

DAPHNE PAPYRACEA, Wall. *Kaghuti, P.*; *Gande, P.*; *Dayshing, Bh.* A large shrub. Very common throughout the forests from 6,000 to 10,000 ft. Fl. 11-2, fr. 5. Fruit red. Wood white, but close-grained and tough. Bark used in the manufacture of paper, of which it gives the common thin yellowish kind. Also for ropes to carry loads, *e.g.* by sawyers to bring out scantlings from the forests. Exceedingly sweet scented.

DAPHNE (WALLICHII, Meissn.). *Chhota Aryili, P.* A common shrub, from about 5,000 ft. altitude almost down to the plains. Used in the manufacture of paper. Fl. 1-2, fr. 5. black.

DAPHNE (LONGIFOLIA, Meissn.). *Shedbarwa, P.* A shrub of hills from 4,000 to 6,000 feet. Fl. 1-2, fr. 11-12, black. Not common. Used in paper manufacture, of which it furnishes the thick, coarse kind.

ARISTOLOCHIACEÆ.

ARISTOLOCHIA ROXBURGHIANA, Klotsch. Twining shrub of L. H. F, from 1,000 to 4,000 ft.; stem up to about 3 in. girth. Fl. 5-6, fr. 12-1.

ARISTOLOCHIA SACCATA, Wall. *Munkungjor, L.*; *Tengalara, P.* Climbing shrub, with stem up to about 3 in. girth from a knotted, swollen rootstock. Terai and up to 6,000 ft. Fl. 3, fr. 7-8. Flowers generally borne on the stem, often in clusters at the root. A very handsome plant.

MYRISTICACEÆ.

MYRISTICA LONGIFOLIA, Wall. E. $\frac{80\text{-}20}{10\text{-}20+2\text{-}3}$ of the Terai M. P. F. *w.* and deep valleys in L. H. F. Wood white; not used. Leaves long, soft, very handsome.

MYRISTICA (perhaps CORTICOSA). Hk. f. and T. A tree of L. H. F., larger than the preceding. Not common.

EUPHORBIACEÆ.

PHYLLANTHUS ANDERSONI. *Latikat, P.* E. $\frac{20\text{-}30}{10\text{-}15+2\text{-}3}$ of L. H. F. valleys. Fl. 3, fr. .

PHYLLANTHUS MULTILOCULARIS, Müll. Arg. *Jagri, P.* E. shrub or small tree, chiefly found along roads and streams in the Terai. Seeds with a bright red arillus.

PHYLLANTHUS THOMSONI. *Latikat, P.* E. $\frac{20\text{-}30}{10\text{-}15+2\text{-}3}$ of Terai and L. H. F. Wood reddish, rather soft, warps easily. Fl. 4-7, fr. 9-10.

PHYLLANTHUS NEPALENSIS, Müll. Arg. E. $\frac{20\text{-}30}{10\text{-}15+2\text{-}3}$. Terai and L. H. F. valleys. Common in Dalka Jhar.

PHYLLANTHUS LANCEOLARIUS, Müll. Arg. *Bangikat, P.*; *Fagiri, L.* E. $\frac{20\text{-}30}{10\text{-}15+2\text{-}3}$. Terai and L. H. F. up to 5,000 ft. Also ascending the valleys. Wood red, hard. Fl. 5-6, fr. 9.

PHYLLANTHUS FAGIFOLIUS, Müll. Arg. *Paili, P.* E. $\frac{20\text{-}30}{10\text{-}15+2\text{-}3}$. Terai M. P. F. *w., e.g.* in Dalka Jhar. Fl. 4. Wood of a yellowish colour, said to be strong.

PHYLLANTHUS BICOLOR, Müll. Arg. *Latikat, P.*; *Tetrikair-kúng, L.*; *Kair-kúng, L.* E. $\frac{40\text{-}50}{10\text{-}20+3\text{-}4}$. U. H. F. from 5,000 to 7,000 ft. Fl. 6, fr. 9. Wood dark red, very hard and strong, but liable to warp unless very well seasoned.

PHYLLANTHUS EMBLICA, Roxb. *Aonla, P.*; *Suom-kúng, P.*; *Owla, M.* L. $\frac{30\text{-}40}{10\text{-}20+2\text{-}3}$ of Terai and L. Hills ascending to 4,000 ft. Fl. 3, fr. 11-12. Fruit eaten. Wood red, hard, with broad medullary rays; not used, as it is only of small size. Fruits edible.

PHYLLANTHUS RETICULATUS, Poiret. L. climbing shrub. Very common along the banks of rivers in the Terai, especially the Mahanadi and Balasun. Fl. fr. 4.

There are also several other species of *Phyllanthus* (section *Glochidion*), of which I have not the names; and even those given are liable to have been wrongly named.

SECURINEGA OBOVATA, Müll. Arg. *Iktibi, L.* Shrub L. $\frac{6\text{-}10}{0+\frac{1}{2}\text{-}1}$ of savannah forests in the Terai. Wood white, close-grained, hard. Fl. 8, fr. 3-4. Leaves eaten by Lepchas.

SECURINEGA (LEUCOPYRUS, Müll. Arg.) *Achal, P.* L. $\frac{10\text{-}20}{0\text{-}5+1\text{-}1\frac{1}{2}}$ on a gravel soil by the banks of rivers in S. K. F., and in bad stony soils up to 4,000 ft., *e.g.* on the southern face of Latpanchor. Wood hard, white, close-grained, with a satiny lustre when cut; might be tried instead of boxwood. Fl. fr 6.

MELANTHESOPSIS PATENS, Müll. Arg. *Ikti-kúng, L.* L. shrub. Common all over the Terai. Fl. fr. 3-4.

Sauropus albicans, Müll. Arg. *Sentungrúng, L.* Shrub. Common in the L. Hills up to 3,000 ft. Fl. fr 9.

Baccaurea sapida, Roxb. *Kalabogati, P.*; *Sumbling-kúng, L.* E. $\frac{30\text{-}40}{10\text{-}15+2\text{-}3}$ of Terai M. P F. *w.* and valleys in L. H. F., generally near rivers. Bark used by Lepchas as a mordant in dyeing with manjit or lac (*Regasu, L*). Fl. 3-4, fr. 5 6; fruit edible.

Bischoffia Javanica, Bl. *Kainjal, P.*; *Sinong-kúng, L.* L. $\frac{40\text{-}60}{20\text{-}30+4\text{-}6}$. L. H. F. valleys and up to 5,000 ft. Occasionally in the Terai near rivers. Very common in the Chenga-Khyrbani forests. Fl. 3. Bark greyish brown. Wood dark crimson, red, with a very strong odour of vinegar. It has a wavy grain, caused by the smaller vessels being arranged in rings parallel to the annual layers. Between these rings are scattered vessels which are much larger. The medullary rays are small. Used occasionally for planking, and by Nepalese for window frames, &c.; it deserves to be much better known.

Antidesma diandrum, Tulasne. *Patimil, P.*; *Kantjer, L.* L. $\frac{10\text{-}20}{5\text{-}8+1\text{-}2}$. Terai and L. H. F., not swampy. Fl. , fr. . Leaves eaten; they resemble sorrel. Wood reddish, hard, close-grained.

Antidesma Bunias, Spreng. *Himalchiri, P.*; *Kautjer, L.* $\frac{L}{E}$ (?) $\frac{10\text{-}20}{5\text{-}10+1\text{-}2}$. Terai and L. H. F. up to 3,000 ft. Fl. , fr. . Leaves and fruit eaten. Wood reddish, hard.

Antidesma Menasu, Müll. Arg. *Kumbyúng, L.*; *Tungcher-kúng, L.* L. $\frac{20\text{-}30}{10\text{-}20+2\text{-}3}$. Terai M. P. F. *w.* and L. H. F. valleys. Fl. 8-9, fr. 12-1. Fruit red, eaten by Lepchas. Wood darkish red, close-grained, strong but liable to warp.

Aporosa dioica, Müll. Arg. L. $\frac{30\text{-}40}{10\text{-}20+2\text{-}3}$. Terai M. P. F. *w., e.g.* Dalka Jhar and L. H. F. valleys. Fl. 2-3, fr. 4-5. Wood red brown, hard.

Aporosa Lindleyana, Wight. *Kagbhalai, P.* E. $\frac{20\text{-}30}{10\text{-}15+2\text{-}3}$ of the M. P. F. *w.* in Terai. Fl. 2-3, fr. .

Cyclostemon subsessile, Kurz. *Bway Champ, P.*; *Asura, P.*; E. $\frac{20\text{-}30}{5\text{-}10+1\text{-}2}$. Deep valleys of the outer hills, *e.g.* near Sivoke. Fl. 12-1, fr. 2-3. Wood yellow-brown, said to resemble that of the Magnolias.

Briedelia retusa, Sprengel. *Geio, P.*; *Pengji-kúng, L.* L. $\frac{40\text{-}50}{20\text{-}30+3\text{-}4}$. Common in Terai S. F., M. P. F. *d.*, and in L. H. F. up to 3,000 ft. Fl. 8, fr. 10. The stems when young have long sharp conical spines, which disappear as the tree gets older. Bark greyish brown when young, darker and deeply fissured vertically when old. Wood yellowish grey, heavy, durable; used for building carts, cattle yokes, &c.: its leaves are cut to feed cattle.

Briedelia stipularis, Bl. *Loima-lara, P.* A large scandent shrub, attaining 1½ to 2 ft. girth. Fl. 8-9, fr. 12-2. Common in M. P. F. *d.* and K. S. F. in Terai and in L. H. F. *r.* up to 2,000 ft. Bark dark brown, deeply fissured. Heartwood very dark brown, hard.

Briedelia montana, Willd. *Geio, P.* L. $\frac{20\text{-}30}{10\text{-}15+2\text{-}3}$ of L. H. F. up to 4,000 ft. Fl. 1-2, fr. 3. Wood resembling that of *B. retusa*. Leaves used to feed cattle.

Briedelia tomentosa, Bl. *Sibri, P.*; *Mantet-kúng, L.* E. $\frac{10\text{-}20}{0\text{-}10+1\text{-}2}$ of M. P. F. *d.* and S. K. F. in Terai and L. H. F. r. up to 2,000 ft. Fl. 9, fr. 10. Wood said to be soft, useless.

Croton caudatus, Müll. Arg. *Tukchabrig, L.* L. climbing shrub, stem reaching often 1 to 1½ ft in girth. Fl. 4-5, fr. 7-8. Found in S. K. F. and M. P. F. *d.* in Terai, and in hills up to 4,000 ft., but most common in waste places. Wood hard and close-grained, bright yellow, turning to white as it gets older; has a strong odour.

Croton oblongifolius, Roxb. *Akh, P.* L. $\frac{30\text{-}40}{10\text{-}20+3\text{-}4}$ of the M. P. F. *d.* and L. H. F. r. up to 2,000 ft Fl. 1. Wood said to be yellow, hard, and close-grained. It gives a small quantity of gum, used by Paharias to cure sores on the legs.

(**Croton polyandrum**, Roxb.) *Poguntig, L.* Shrub $\frac{4\text{-}6}{0+\frac{1}{4}\text{-}\frac{1}{2}}$ of the M. and U. H. F. Common about Tukdah and Hoom. Fl. 8, fr.

Trewia nudiflora, Linn. *Garum, P.*;* *Gamari, P.*;* *Tung-flam-kúng, L.* L. $\frac{30\text{-}40}{15\text{-}20+3\text{-}4}$ of M. P. F. *d.* and S. K. F. in Terai, and to 2,000 ft. in L. H. F., but seems chiefly to be found on roadsides and waste places. Fl. 2-3, fr. 6-7. Wood yellowish white, soft, used to make cattle troughs. The Pahari names [*] seem chiefly to be given from a resemblance of the leaves to those of *Gmelina arborea* and *Adina cordifolia*.

Cleidion Javanicum, Bl. *Palap-kúng, L.* E. $\frac{40\text{-}60}{10\text{-}20+4\text{-}5}$ of the L. H. F. valleys up to 1,000 ft. Fl. 1, fr. 6.

Mallotus Philippinensis, Müll. Arg *Sindooria, P.*; *Puroa-kúng, L.* E. $\frac{20\text{-}30}{10\text{-}15+2\text{-}3}$ of M. P. F. *d.* and S. F. in Terai and S. F. and L. H. F. up to 4,000 feet in hills. Fl. 7-8, fr 1-2. Wood reddish brown, hard, close-grained. Fruit covered with a red powder (*kamila*), used as a dye, but rarely. The tree is better known by the old name, *Rottlera tinctoria, Roxb.*

Mallotus (**Helferi**, Müll. Arg.). E $\frac{20\text{-}25}{6\text{-}10+1\text{-}2}$ of M. P. F. *w.* in Terai; only found by me in the Dalka Jhar.

Mallotus albus, Müll. Arg. *Jogi Mallata, P.*; *Numbong-kúng, L.* E. $\frac{20\text{-}30}{10\text{-}15+2\text{-}3}$ of L. H. F. valleys in inner hills, and in M. H. F. to 5,000 feet. Fl. 5, fr. 8. Capsule 4-seeded (called *M. tetracoccus* in Kurz's *Burma Flora*). Wood white, soft, much attacked by insects.

Mallotus Roxburghianus, Müll. Arg. *Kamli Mallata, P.*; *Phusri Mallata, P.* E. $\frac{10\text{-}20}{5\text{-}10+\frac{1}{2}\text{-}1}$ of L. H. F. damp valleys. Fl. 7. Wood hard, white, close-grained, resembles boxwood.

Mallotus oreophilus, Müll. Arg. *Numboongkor, L.* L. $\frac{20\text{-}30}{10\text{-}15+1\text{-}2}$ of U. H. F. from 5,000 to 8,000 ft. Common about Darjeeling. Fl. 7, fr. 9.

MALLOTUS, SP. *Kamli Mallata, P.; Namjil, L.* $\frac{L}{E}$ (?) $\frac{10\text{-}20}{5\text{-}10+1\text{-}1\frac{1}{2}}$ of L. H. F. valleys. Common along the Tista river.

MACARANGA (DENTICULATA, Müll. Arg.). *Mallata, P.; Numrokúng, L.* E. $\frac{40\text{-}60}{20\text{-}30+3\text{-}4}$. M. H. F. from 3,000 to 6,000 ft. Chiefly, or almost entirely, on land which has been once cleared, and on which it is almost always the first forest crop: thus in some places, *e.g.* at Hoom-Linding, Tukdah, Pugraingbong and Paiengaon near Dumsong, forming almost of itself the forest. It is very fast growing. In ten years it grows 40 ft. high with 3 ft. girth; and as its shade is light, it acts as a nurse to better kinds of trees, such as toon, walnut, or chestnut. Fl. 10-11, fr. 4. Leaves *not* peltate, triangular, ovate acuminate. Wood white, prettily grained, but not durable; would do for tea-boxes. Used for fences for their fields by the Lepchas and Bhutias on account of its long straight stems.

MACARANGA (GUMMIFLUA, Müll. Arg.). *Jogi Mallata, P.* E. $\frac{30\text{-}40}{20\text{-}30+3\text{-}4}$. M. H. F. in similar places to the above, but not so common, and generally on southern slopes. Easily distinguished by its broadly peltate leaves. A copious red clear gum exudes wherever a branch, or even leaf, is cut.

MACARANGA INDICA, Müll. Arg. *Dagdakti, M.; Lal Mallata, P.* E. $\frac{20\text{-}30}{10\text{-}15+2\text{-}3}$. Terai M. P. F. *w.* and L. H. F. up to 3,000 ft. Wood greyish white, soft, not durable. Fl. , fr. .

MACARANGA, SP. *Sing-kúng, L.* L. $\frac{20\text{-}30}{10\text{-}15+2\text{-}3}$. M. H. F., especially old cultivation. Very common about Tukdah and Hoom-Linding. Fl. fr. never seen. The leaves turn a bright golden red before falling in December. They are used by Lepchas to poison fish, and their juice is said to raise blisters if applied to the skin.

ALCHORNEA TILIÆFOLIA, Müll. Arg. *Chhota Kagshi, P.* E. $\frac{10\text{-}15}{0\text{-}5+\frac{1}{2}\text{-}1}$ of the L. and M. H. F. from 2,000 to 5,000 ft. Very common on Latpanchor ridge.

RICINUS COMMUNIS, Linn. *Orer, P.; Rajlak-kúng, L.* The castor oil plant. E. $\frac{10\text{-}15}{0\text{-}5+\frac{1}{2}\text{-}1}$. Comes up in great abundance in old cultivations. It is cultivated by Mechis to feed silkworms with the leaves.

JATROPHA CURCAS, Linn. *Bagverendi, B. H.; Kadam, P.* E. $\frac{10\text{-}15}{0\text{-}10+1\text{-}2}$. Often found in old village sites, and is used in the Terai for hedges. Wood very soft, white. Seeds used as a purgative.

HOMONOYA RIPARIA, Lour. *Khola Ruis, P.; Mongthel-kúng, L.* E. small shrub, its stem reaching 6 in. in girth. Common along the beds of the Rangít and Tista rivers during their whole course in the district, but never seen by me on any other of the rivers, such as the Balasun or Mechi. Wood pink-white.

HOMONOYA SYMPHYLLIÆFOLIA, Kurz. *Jagrikat, P.; Chingkúng, L.* E. $\frac{20\text{-}40}{10\text{-}15+2\text{-}3}$ of the damp forests of the L. H. Very common in the Tista valley, especially near Sivoke. Fl. 4, fr. 10. Bark thin, white; peels off in flakes. The section of the stem is very irregular, somewhat resembling that of the hornbeam, but with deeper sinuosities. It is one of the hardest woods in the district, very close-grained, even, works easily, and should be tried as a substitute for boxwood. Bengali boatmen carry it away eagerly when they find it adrift in the Tista to make poles to work their boats up stream. It is said to grow to a very large size in Nepal, where it is used for boats, and is largely sold from depôt. (The statements of the Nepalese may perhaps relate to some other tree, but cannot be verified without specimens.)

OSTODES PANICULATA, Bl. *Mya, P.*; *Bepari, P.*; *Palok-kúng, L.* E. $\frac{50\text{-}60}{20\text{-}30+6\text{-}8}$ of M. H. F., ascending to 6,000 ft. and descending to 2,000 ft. Fl. 6, fr. 11. It gives a gum, which is used as a size in the manufacture of paper. The wood is white, soft; not used

EXCÆCARIA BACCATA, Müll Arg. *Pudlikat, P.*; *Lal Kain-jal,* P. L. $\frac{40\text{-}60}{20\text{-}30+4\text{-}6}$ of the M. P. F. *w.* of Terai and L. H. F. valleys. Common in Dalka Jhar and near Sivoke. When in young foliage, in April, has a very handsome appearance, the leaves being then of an orange-red colour. Fl. 4. Wood said to resemble that of *Bischoffia Javanica.*

EUPHORBIA (NERIIFOLIA, L.). L. $\frac{10\text{-}20}{5\text{-}10+2\text{-}3}$. Cultivated as a sacred tree by the Mechis, who guard it most carefully, making a fence round it; consequently it is often found on the sites of old Mechi villages grown into a tree.

EUPHORBIA (POINSETTIA) PULCHERRIMA, Willd., is a shrub with showy crimson floral leaves, not uncommon in gardens.

SARCOCOCCA SALIGNA, Don. *Chilikat, P.* Shrub $\frac{6\text{-}8}{0\text{-}4+\frac{1}{2}\text{-}\frac{3}{4}}$ of the U. H. F. from 6,000 to 9,000 ft. Not very common. Fl. 10, fr. 11. Wood hard, like boxwood; used for walking-sticks.

URTICACEÆ.

ULMUS LANCIFOLIA, Roxb. *Lapi, P.* L. $\frac{60\text{-}80}{30\text{-}40+8\text{-}10}$ of the L. H. F. valleys up to 2,000 feet. Fl. fr. 3.

CELTIS TETRANDRA, Roxb. *Koomsoong-kúng, L.* L. $\frac{60\text{-}80}{20\text{-}30+6\text{-}10}$ of the L. H. F. valleys. Common along the Tista and Great Rangít rivers. Fl. 2, fr. .

CELTIS TRINERVIA, Roxb. *Sedongtagla, L.* L. $\frac{30\text{-}40}{10\text{-}20+3\text{-}4}$ (?) of the L. H. F. and inner valleys. Fl. 3-4, fr. 6-7.

SPONIA POLITORIA, Planch. *Kooail, P.*; *Tuksat-kúng, L.* E. $\frac{20\text{-}30}{10\text{-}15+2\text{-}3}$. Common in L. H. F., especially in old cultivated land. Fl. 6-7. Wood light, reddish brown with darker coloured medullary rays, soft, easily decaying. The bark is used to tie up the rafters of native houses and to make temporary ropes for all purposes. Distinguished from the next by its leaves being very rough and green beneath.

SPONIA ORIENTALIS, Planch. *Kooail, P.*; *Tugla-kúng, L.* E. $\frac{20\text{-}30}{10\text{-}15+2\text{-}4}$. Common in Terai and L. H. F., especially in old cultivations, where it comes up in great quantity. Very fast growing. One tree cut down in front of the Sivoke resthouse had attained a girth of about 40 in. and a height of 25 feet in five years. Bark grey-brown, rough, with innumerable lenticels. Wood like the preceding, and bark used for the same purposes. Leaves densely covered with soft grey hairs beneath.

(GIRONNIERA THOMSONI, King.) *Lali, P.* E. $\frac{60\text{-}80}{30\text{-}40+8\text{-}12}$ of the U. H. F. from 6,000 to 8,000 ft. Fl. fr. I have never found in spite of constant search. Wood red-brown, close-grained, much used for planking, rafters, &c. (This is the true "Lali" of the Paharias, but in the station of Darjeeling a species of laurel is often called "Lali," viz. *Machilus odoratissimus.*)

GIRONNIERA, SP. *Sionsoon-kúng, L.* Tree of the L. H. F. and inner valleys. Fl. fr. 6.

ARTOCARPUS INTEGRIFOLIA, Linn. *Kuttal, Bg.* The jack tree. Cultivated all over the Terai and in the lower part of the hills. Wood bright yellow, turning brown with age; very handsome.

ARTOCARPUS LAKOOCHA, Roxb. *Dehua, Bg.* A handsome tree, occasionally found planted near villages in the Terai. Wood similar to the above, but of a much darker colour.

ARTOCARPUS CHAPLASHA, Roxb. *Lut-ter, P.* L. $\frac{80\text{-}120}{50\text{-}60+10\text{-}12}$. Common in the Terai M. P. F. *w.* (especially the Dalka Jhar) and in the L. H. F. and M. H. F. valleys, ascending up to nearly 5,000 ft. Fine specimens may be seen in the Rungjo valley below the cinchona plantation and below Pankabari. A very handsome tree with its tall straight stem and large broad leaves. Fl. 3, fr.? The wood is bright yellow, turning brown with exposure. Much lighter and looser grained than that of the jack tree, but easily worked and very useful for furniture and planking. It is also used for dug-outs on the Tista river. When young the leaves are often 2 ft. in length and pinnatifid, resembling in shape a huge leaf of *Quercus robur.*

CUDRANIA JAVANENSIS, Trécul. A large shrub or small tree of the Terai and Duars, chiefly in hedges or isolated in the cultivated portion.

STREBLUS ASPER, Lour. *Siora, H. Bg.* E. $\frac{30\text{-}40}{15\text{-}20+3\text{-}4}$ of the L. H. F. and of the cultivated parts of the Terai near villages. Not common. Leaves very rough. Fl. 3-4, fr. 6-7.

FICUS BENGALENSIS, Linn. *Bor, H.*; *Kungji-kúng, L.*; *Borhar, P.* E. $\frac{60\text{-}80}{20\text{-}30+}$?). The banyan. Wild all over the M. P. F. *w.* of Terai and L. H. F. and cultivated in the Terai, especially on roadsides. The largest of all the species except, perhaps, the India-rubber fig. It generally grows epiphytically on some other tree, and sends down multitudes of aërial roots from the branches, but less in the forest than in the open. Wood soft, but tough; not used. Recognized by its large, somewhat one-sided, leaves, red fruit and grey horizontally furrowed bark.

FICUS MYSORENSIS, Roth. *Sunkong-kúng, L.* E. 40-50. Generally a large epiphytic tree, but not common, in L. H. F.

up to 3,000 ft. Fr. 4. Distinguished by its parallel veined soft leaves, generally about 1 ft. long, and large fruit.

FICUS LACCIFERA, Bth. *Yokdung, L.* E. 70-80. Generally epiphytic in the M. P. F. *d.* of Terai and L. H. F. valleys, *e.g.* in Sivoke Hills and Pursam Jhora. Very large tree; gives India-rubber, but more sparingly, and of not so good quality as the *F. elastica.*

FICUS ALTISSIMA, Bl. E. epiphytic in the M. P. F. *w.* of Terai (*e.g.* Dalka Jhar). Large tree, gives a milky juice resembling India-rubber.

FICUS OBTUSIFOLIA, Roxb. E. Generally epiphytic. 60-80 ft. (The height of all the epiphytic figs depends, of course, on that of the tree they grow upon.) M. P. F. *w.* in Terai and L. H. F. Distinguished by its leaves being similar in shape to those of *F. laccifera*, and having more or less the venation of *F. elastica.* They are sharply cuneate at the base and obtuse at the summit. The fruit is small and dotted with red specks. It gives an India-rubber of inferior quality.

FICUS COMOSA, Roxb. *Kunhip, L.* E. $\frac{40\text{-}50}{10\text{-}20 + 3\text{-}4}$ if on its own roots. but often epiphytic. One of the prettiest of the figs. Distinguished by its small oval parallel-veined leaves and big green fruit. Fr 3.

FICUS THOMSONI, Miq. Tree, generally epiphytic, of the L. H. F. and inner valleys. Fr. 9. Distinguished by its small fruit, leaves tomentose beneath, and prominent basal nerves not parallel to the remainder.

FICUS ELASTICA, Bl. *Bor, H. Bg.*; *Lesoo, P.*; *Yok, L.* E., generally epiphytic, of the L. H. F. up to 2,000 ft. Not seen in the plains or in hills west of the Mahanadi, except on that river itself or its tributaries. It is the true Indian India-rubber, but in Darjeeling it is quite at its western limit. There are magnificent specimens in the Tista and Great Rangít valleys, of immense height, with thousands of aërial roots. The trees have not been tapped the last two years. as it was found necessary to give them rest, they having been so much overtapped before that that a large number had died off. It has been very successfully propagated from seed at Bamunpokri, where about one acre has been planted 5′ × 5′ direct, and some hundreds of plants fixed in the forks of useless trees in rush baskets. Most of these have sent out roots, which may be seen making their way down the stem of the tree; and there is no doubt but that this system of propagation will succeed admirably. The tree may also be easily propagated from cuttings; but these should not be of old wood, but of young fleshy shoots. The best plan to obtain these is to pollard a few branches, and the shoots are then sent out in profusion. The wood is yellowish brown, tough, but not durable. It is not used. The annual rings are very indistinct, owing to the concentric rings of alternate light and dark tissue. The leaves are large, very handsome and easily recognized; the fruit small, brown, spotted, oblong—ripe 9-10 The stem is easily recognized in the forests by the reddish brown scurfy stem and aërial roots, and by the strong odour of fresh India-rubber, which is often perceptible from a considerable distance

Ficus retusa, Linn. *Jamu, P.*; *Sitnyok L.* Large tree, generally epiphytic. M. P. F. and S. F. of Terai and L. H. F. Fr. 6 Leaves small, and figs about the size of a small pea.

Ficus infectoria, Willd. *Sefed kabra, P.*; *Kungji-kúng. L.* L. large tree, generally epiphytic, of the S. F. and M. P. F. *d.* and *w.* of Terai and L. H F. in dryer localities generally. Common in sâl forests. Fr. 6. Often planted for ornament in the Terai near villages and on roadsides. Recognized by its long petioled leaves, small fruit, and light grey shining bark.

Ficus cordifolia, Roxb. *Pakur.* Large tree, generally epiphytic, of S. F. and M. P. F. in Terai and L. H. F. Not very common.

Ficus religiosa, Linn. *Pipal, H.*; *Pipli, P.* Very large tree, only cultivated near villages and along roadsides in the Terai. Fr. 11-12. Recognized by its poplar-like, long acuminate leaves.

Ficus pisifera, Wall. *Lekbilani, P* E ? $\frac{20-30}{10-15+2-3}$ of L. H. F. up to 3,000 ft. Fr 5.

Ficus gemella, Wall. *Dudila, P.*; *Toltjay, L.* E. $\frac{30-50}{10-20+3-4}$ of U. H. F. from 6,000 to 8,000 ft. Fr. 6. Leaves used to feed cattle.

Ficus scandens, Roxb. Trailing shrub growing on rocks from 3,000 to 5,000 ft. Fr. 8.

Ficus foveolata, Wall. *Dudila-lara, P.*; *Taksotrig.* L. large climbing shrub of U. H. F., from 5,000 to 8,000 ft. Very common about Darjeeling. Fr. 5.

Ficus monticola. Miq. *Dudila, P.*; *Tshithé, L.* L. ? $\frac{30-40}{10-20+2-3}$ of U. H F. from 6,000 to 8,000 ft. Fr. 5. Leaves used to feed cattle. Wood said to be strong but not durable.

Ficus clavata, Wall. *Girulee, P.*; *Siratpé, L.* E. ? $\frac{15-20}{5-10+\frac{1}{2}-1}$ of M P. F. *w.* in Terai, L. H F. valleys and M H F. up to 5,000 ft. Fr. 2 3. Wood rather heavy. Bark greenish black. Leaves used to feed cattle.

Ficus cyrtophylla *Kasirut, P.*; *Tuksot-kúng, L.* L. ? $\frac{15-20}{5-10+1-2}$ of M. P. F., L. and M. H. F. up to 5,000 ft. Fr. 5. Leaves very rough. Bark used to make ropes by Paharias.

Ficus macrophylla, Roxb. *Kasrekan, P.*; *Kundoung-kúng, L.* E. $\frac{20-30}{10-15+2-3}$ of Terai, banks of streams, L H. and M. H. F. up to 6,000 ft. Common in abandoned cultivations. Fruit pear-shaped, large, edible. Fr. 4.

Ficus Roxburghii, Miq. *Kasreto, P.*; *Gyasay-kúng, L.* E. $\frac{20-30}{0-15+2-3}$ of Terai, L. and M. H. F. up to 5,000 ft. Very handsome with its soft big leaves and reddish edible fruit, covered with golden-coloured hairs. Fr. 8.

Ficus glomerata, Roxb. *Gular, H.*; *Dumri P.*; *Tchongtay-kúng, L.* E. $\frac{20\text{-}30}{10\text{-}15+2\text{-}3}$ of Terai and L. H. F. Not common. Fr. 3, edible; good elephant *charra.*

Ficus (Chittagonga, Miq.). *Dumriphal, P.* E. $\frac{15\text{-}20}{5\text{-}10+1\text{-}2}$? of M. P. F., especially banks of streams; in Terai fruit edible.

Ficus regia, Miq. *Timil, P.*; *Tchongtay-kúng, L.* E. $\frac{20\text{-}30}{5\text{-}10+2\text{-}3}$ of L. H. F. and M. P. F. *d.* in Terai. Fruit edible (perhaps the best of the wild edible kinds). There is a fine tree close to the spring at Bamunpokri.

Ficus hispida, Linn. Fil. *Kharwa, P.*; *Tuksot-kúng, L.* E. $\frac{30\text{-}40}{5\text{-}15+3\text{-}4}$ of M. P. F. *d.* in Terai and L. H. F. up to 4,000 ft. Very common in waste places, on the banks of streams in the Terai and in abandoned cultivations in hills. Good elephant fodder. Fruit edible. Big trees may be seen at Bamunpokri and Chenga. Easily recognized by its opposite leaves and hollow stems. Fr 1-2.

Ficus pyriformis, Hk. and Arn. *Sani dudila, P.*; *Payo-kúng, L.* Shrub or small tree. Common all over the district from the Terai to 8,000 ft. Leaves long acuminate, glabrous.

Ficus Cunia, Buch. *Kanhya, P.*; *Kauai, M.*; *Sungji-kúng, L.* E $\frac{30\text{-}40}{6\text{-}10+3\text{-}4}$ of Terai M. P. F. *d.* and L. H. F. up to 2,000 ft. Very common. Fruit edible. Bark used to tie the rafters of native houses. Easily recognized by its unequal semicordate leaves and long leafless racemes of fruit from the lower part of the stem. Fr. 5-6.

Böhmeria rugulosa, Wedd. *Dar, P.*; *Sedeng, L.* E. $\frac{20\text{-}30}{10\text{-}15+3\text{-}4}$ of the L. H. F., especially dry exposures Very common in the upper part of Chenga forest Fl. 3, fr. 11. Wood much esteemed, dark red, heavy, with fine medullary rays.

Böhmeria platyphylla, Don. *Kamli, P.*; *Dangnoxooketek, L.* L. shrub E. of the M. F. P. Terai, L. M. and U. H. F. up to 7,000 ft. The variety *macrostachya* is generally found up to 5,000 ft., above that is found the variety *rotundifolia*, which is common in Darjeeling. Fibre used to make ropes. Fl. 8.

Böhmeria polystachya, Wedd. *Phusre kamli*; *Taksur, L.* L. shrub of U. Hills Common round Darjeeling, 7,000 ft. Fl. 8. Gives a fibre; not used.

Böhmeria macrophylla, Don *Kamli, P.*; *Pua,* E. $\frac{10\text{-}15}{0\text{-}5+\frac{1}{2}\text{-}\frac{1}{4}}$ of the L. H. F., especially by banks of streams, often found in K. S. F. in Terai. Fibre used to make ropes and fishing-lines. Fl. 8, fr. 11.

Böhmeria Malabarica, Wedd. *Takbret-kúng, L.* E. $\frac{15\text{-}20}{0+\frac{1}{2}\text{-}\frac{1}{4}}$ of the L. and M. H F., forming an undergrowth up to 5,000 ft. Fibre used for ropes. Fl. 3.

Böhmeria Hamiltoniana, Wedd. *Taksur, L.* E. $\frac{10\text{-}15}{0+\frac{1}{2}\text{-}\frac{1}{4}}$ of the L. and M. H. F. up to 5,000 ft. Fibre used for ropes. Fl. 10.

MAOUTIA PUYA. Wedd. *Puya, P.*; *Kyinki, L.* E. 6-10. Waste places and abandoned cultivation in Terai and L. Hills up to 4,000 ft. The fibre is extensively used to make ropes, cloth, fishing nets, &c.

POUZOLZIA VIMINEA, Wedd. (1) *Chhota kooail, P.*; *Kyingbi, L.* E. $\frac{10\text{-}20}{0\text{-}5+\frac{1}{2}\text{-}1}$ of beds of streams in Terai and in L. H. F. up to 5,000 ft. Common in abandoned cultivations, where it grows into a small tree. Leaves eaten by Lepchas Bark used for ropes. Wood brown-yellow, soft, but heavy. Warps easily.

Lilima, P. (2) This variety is common at 7,000 ft., especially about the station of Darjeeling, and is a large, much branched shrub.

LAPORTEA CRENULATA, Gaudich. *Moringi, P.*; *Sunkrong, L.* E. $\frac{15\text{-}20}{5\text{-}10+1\text{-}2}$ of M. P. F. *w.* in Terai and L. H. F. up to 4,000 ft. Fl. fr. 1. Fibre good for rope, but the preparation has a poisonous effect. Leaves and young shoots have poisonous, stinging hairs, the effects of which are very painful, lasting very long.

URTICA HETEROPHYLLA, Willd. *Ullo, P.*; *Kasu, L.* A shrub or shrubby herb of the M. and U. H F., forming a dense undergrowth in some forests from 3,000 to 8,000 ft It has very long stinging hairs, the effects of which are, however, not lasting. The fibre is used for ropes, twine, &c., and for coarse cloth, like gunny, to make bags.

VILLEBRUNEA FRUTESCENS, BL. *Kirma, P.*; *Takbret-kúng, L.* E. $\frac{15\text{-}20}{5\text{-}10+\frac{1}{2}\text{-}1}$ of the M. P. F. *w.* of Terai and L. H. F. valleys up to 4,000 ft. Fibre used for ropes.

VILLEBRUNEA APPENDICULATA, Wedd. *Lipic, P.*; *Kaphitki, L.* E. $\frac{20\text{-}30}{10\text{-}15+1\text{-}2}$ of the L. H. F. up to 4,000 ft. Fibre used to make ropes, nets, and coarse cloth. It has a brownish colour. Fl. 2-3.

DEBREGEASIA LONGIFOLIA, Wedd. *Tushari, P*; *Kamhyem-kúng, L.* E. $\frac{20\text{-}30}{10\text{-}15+2\text{-}3}$ of the M. and U. H. F. from 4,000 to 7,000 ft. Wood when old reddish black. Fibre used to make ropes, and fishing-nets.

DEBREGEASIA. *Poorooni, P.*; *Senén-kúng, L.* Big climber of the M. and U H. F. from 4,000 to 7,000 ft Very handsome with its big round cordate leaves snow-white beneath. Fl. 5-6, Fruit edible.

CONOCEPHALUS SUAVEOLENS, Bl. *Gulsuné, P.* Big climber of M. P. F. *w.* in Terai and L. H. F. valleys. Fl. 2-3.

CONOCEPHALUS, SP. *Kusrit, P.* Big climber of L. H. F. valleys. Fl. 2-3.

MORUS SERRATA. Roxb. *Kimbu, P.*; *Numbyong-kúng, L.*; *Singtok, Bh.* L. $\frac{100\text{-}120}{50\text{-}60+10\text{-}15}$ of the L. H. F. valleys and in the inner ranges. Common in the Great Rangít valley. Fl. 3, fr. 9-10. Wood yellowish brown; very good for house-building.

MORUS INDICA, L. *Chhota Kimbu, P.*; *Mekrup-kúng, L.* L $\frac{10\text{-}20}{0\text{-}5+1\text{-}2}$ of the valleys and up to 4,000 ft. Very common along the Tista. Fl. 2-3, fr. 9-10. Fruit edible.

CUPULIFERÆ.

QUERCUS LAMELLOSA, Sm. *Budgrat, P.*; *Búk, L.* $\frac{100\text{-}120}{30\text{-}40+15\text{-}20}$. The big Darjeeling oak, commonly called "Búk," and found in the U. H. F. from 6,000 to 9,000 ft. Fl 4-5, fr. 11. Bark grey-brown with rough spots. The wood is hard, heavy, with very broad medullary rays. The sapwood is white, and decays easily; the heart-wood brown, often with bands of an almost black colour, and durable if not too much exposed to wet. When cut in the direction of the medullary rays it is very handsome, and deserves to be more used than it is in cabinet-work. The large vessels are chiefly arranged in wavy lines parallel to the medullary rays, and the annual rings are very indistinct and difficult to count. The wood is used for beams, door-posts, rafters, &c., and it is a very good firewood. It splits well, and is occasionally used for shingles. After an age of about 100 to 120 years the tree generally becomes hollow in the centre, at the same time as it still increases in girth, so that ancient trees of 20 to 30 ft. or more are often found in the old forests. The chief forests west of the Tista, in which this oak predominates, are those on the big spurs of Senchul, Gumpahar, Mahalderam, and Tukdah.

QUERCUS ANNULATA, Sm. *Phalat, P.*; *Siri-kúng, L.* E. $\frac{100\text{-}120}{30\text{-}40+12\text{-}15}$ of the U. H. F. from 6,000 to 9,000 ft. Fl. 4-5, fr. 9-10. Bark similar to that of *Q. lamellosa.* Wood also like the wood of that tree, but its colour is more variegated with darker and lighter bands. It is used for the same purposes, but is much more liable to shrink and warp.

QUERCUS (ACUMINATA, Roxb.). *Chhota Arkoulo, P.* E. $\frac{30\text{-}40}{15\text{-}20+3\text{-}4}$ of the U. H. F. from 5,000 to 7,000 ft. Not very common, but found with *Q. fenstrata.* Fr. 12-1. Fine specimens may be seen on the Birch Hill Road, Darjeeling. Wood reddish yellow, close-grained, with fine medullary rays and pores in short wavy lines.

QUERCUS SPICATA, Sm. *Arkoulo, P.*; *Kucheeng-kúng, L.* E. $\frac{40\text{-}60}{20\text{-}30+3\text{-}5}$ of the M. P. F. *w.* in Terai (Dalka Jhar, common) L. H. F. valleys and M. H. F. up to 5,000 ft. Fl. 3-4, fr. 9-10 of second year. Wood not used. It coppices very freely, is of quick growth, and would probably be worth growing in coppice by planters mixed with chestnut for firewood and charcoal.

QUERCUS (FENESTRATA, Roxb.). *Patlé katús, P*; *Kashiendúng, L.* E $\frac{30\text{-}40}{15\text{-}20+3\text{-}4}$ of the U. H. F. from 5,000 to 7,000 ft. Not so common as *Q. lamellosa* or *annulata.* Fl. 3, fr. 12-1. It is chiefly found in the forests about 5,000 to 6,000 ft., *e.g.* at Tukdah and Dumsong.

QUERCUS PACHYPHYLLA, Kurz. *Bara katús, P.*; *Hloserie-kúng, L.* E. $\frac{80\text{-}120}{30\text{-}40+12\text{-}15}$ of the U. H. F. from 6,000 to 10,000 ft. Fl. ?, fr. 11. It is common round Senchul and Gumpahar, but its chief locality is in the forests of the Singalila range, especially round

Tongloo. Wood yellowish white, hard, much lighter than that of *Q. lamellosa*, with very fine or almost no medullary rays; more durable in water than the wood of *Q. lamellosa*, and preferred for palings, shingles, and planking. Fruit in a compact mass, the cups being joined together generally in threes.

QUERCUS LANCEÆFOLIA, Roxb. *Patlé katús, P.*; *Siri-kúng, L.* E. $\frac{30\text{-}40}{15\text{-}20+3\text{-}4}$ of the Terai (banks of streams) L. and M. H. F. up 5,000 ft. Fl. 2-3, fr. 9. Wood resembling that of the preceding, with very fine medullary rays. The fruit has thin broad-ringed cups, which are set sideways on the branch, and the kernel has ruminate albumen. It is used as a bait to catch birds, who appear to be fond of it.

CASTANOPSIS INDICA, A. DC. *Banj katús, P.*; *Kashiorón. L.* E. $\frac{20\text{-}40}{10\text{-}20+3\text{-}5}$ of the M. P. F. *w.* Terai, L. H. F. and M. H. F. to 6,000 ft., but commonest in the latter. Fl. 11-12. fr. 9 10. Comes up generally on old cultivated lands about 4,000 ft. on dry exposures. Wood greyish white, splits easily, much used for shingles, which may be the reason that so few big trees are ever found. A few may, however, be seen east of the Tista. About Kalimpung it, as well as the next species, are kept standing in the fields and pollarded to be burnt for manure. The fruit is about the size of a filbert, which it rather resembles in flavour.

CASTANOPSIS TRIBULOIDES, A. DC *Mueré katús, P.*; *Kashioshem, L.* E. $\frac{30\text{-}50}{15\text{-}20+4\text{-}5}$ of the same localities as the preceding. Fl. 3 4, fr. 9-10. Wood greyish brown, with rather broad medullary rays; much used for house-building, shingles, &c. Fruit edible.

CASTANOPSIS ARGENTEA, Bl. *Kuchiang-kúng, L.* L.? Tree of the M. P. F. *w.* and banks of streams in Terai and L Hills.

CASTANOPSIS RUFESCENS, Hk. f. and T. *Dalné katús, P.*; *Sirikishu, L.* E. $\frac{100\text{-}120}{30\text{-}50+10\text{-}20}$ of the U. H. F. from 6,000 to 8,000 ft. Common about Darjeeling. Fl. 5, fr. 9-10. Wood almost exactly like that of *Q. pachyphylla*, and used for the same purposes. Fruit very long—prickly, the largest of the Darjeeling species; edible.

(CORYLUS FEROX, Wall.) A small tree of the forests of the Singalila range above 8,000 ft.

BETULACEÆ.

BETULA BHOJPATTRA, Wall. *Takpa, Bh.* L. $\frac{40\text{-}60}{20\text{-}30+3\text{-}4}$. Found on the Singalila Ridge from 9,000 to 12,000 ft. Some very large specimens below Tongloo on the path to Surmonbong and Kinjalia. Bark white. Wood very close-grained, white and strong.

BETULA ACUMINATA, Wall. *Saver, P.*; *Payúng, P.*; *Hlosonlikúng, L.* L. $\frac{30\text{-}40}{20\text{-}30+2\text{-}3}$. Common round Darjeeling, and especially about Birch Hill. Fl. 3-4, fr. 5-6. Bark grey, silvery, papery, peeling off in horizontal strips and marked with big lenticels. Wood white or slightly brownish white, with numerous medullary rays and broad annual rings; takes a polish; works well. Softer than that of *B. Bhojpattra.*

BETULA CYLINDROSTACHYS, Wall. *Sauer, P.*; *Sungli-kúng, L.* L. $\frac{80\text{-}100}{40\text{-}60+6\text{-}8}$. A very large and handsome tree of M. H. F. from 3,000 to 6,000 ft., but found occasionally even in the Terai; it has pendent branchlets. Fl. 12. Wood very hard and good, but not used, though it is better than many other woods in constant use in the district; it is of a reddish colour with a rather twisted grain. Bark pink, peeling off in large flakes and vertically, giving a shaggy appearance to the stem.

ALNUS NEPALENSIS, D. Don. *Utis, P.* L. $\frac{80\text{-}100}{30\text{-}40+6\text{-}10}$. A large tree of the M. H. F. from 3,000 to 6,000 ft., but often extending still higher up. Common round Darjeeling. Is often found in second growth forest in old cultivations, especially near streams. Fl. 9-10, fr. 12-1. In the forest the bark has a dark green colour, and the tree is easily recognized; in open places it is generally silvery grey, resembling that of the birch. Stem very cylindrical, tall, grows very rapidly. Wood yellow-white, almost orange in the older circles of the annual rings, medullary rays broad, each ending in the liber in a horny plate; soft, light, easily worked, does not warp or split; it is rarely used though it deserves to be extensively employed for tea-boxes and for other purposes for which a light wood which does not warp is required.

JUGLANDACEÆ.

JUGLANS REGIA, Linn. *Akrot*; *Kowal kúng, L.* L. $\frac{80\text{-}100}{30\text{-}40+8\text{-}12}$. The walnut. Found in the M. H. F., especially in ravines, between 3,000 and 5,000 ft. altitude. Is now rather scarce, as are most of the trees of the 3,000 to 6,000 ft. zone, that being the zone of Lepcha cultivation; but it has already been planted successfully at Rungbool, and large nurseries are being made at that place and Rungyrúm. At the latter place a few old trees still remain, and the walnut will probably succeed admirably. In the Tukdah reserve are many fine trees, especially on the Rungbong Johra and above Mangwa. Fl. 3-4, fr. 9-11. Bark grey, deeply fissured vertically. Wood dark greyish brown, more uniformly and less handsomely marked than the walnut wood in Europe: it also seems lighter and not so close-grained. It is the most valuable wood of the hills, and was very extensively used in house building until its scarcity and the distance at which it had to be sought rendered it too expensive. Many houses, and notably the inspection bungalow at Rungbi; have nearly all their wood work of walnut. It is also occasionally used for shingles by Bhutias, as it splits easily; but for this purpose it is probably not so good as chestnut. The nuts have a very hard shell, but are largely collected. Most of the walnuts, however, sold in Darjeeling or exported to the plains come from the Raja of Sikkim's territory. A remarkable thing is the percentage of good nuts: out of thousands sown at Rungbool scarcely one in a hundred failed to germinate.

ENGELHARDTIA SPICATA, Bl. *Mowa, Mahua, P.*; *Suviak-kúng, L.* L. $\frac{60\text{-}100}{30\text{-}50+8\text{-}12}$. A very large handsome tree of the M. H. F., spreading down to the plains, and often found even in the Terai (Sukna, Dalka Jhar). Very handsome in the winter, when covered with its long drooping catkins and winged seeds resembling those of the hornbeam. Bark grey. Stem cylindrical. Wood much used for house-building, tea-boxes, &c. It is of a pink-grey colour, and has a satiny lustre. It has fine medullary rays and large vessels, and works easily. It coppices freely, as may be seen in the coppice woods at Nagri, and seedlings come up profusely wherever they get sufficient light and protection from cattle. Fl. 9-10, fr. 11-12.

SALICACEÆ.

SALIX TETRASPERMA, Roxb. *Beis, M. H.* E. $\frac{20\text{-}30}{5\text{-}10+2\text{-}3}$. Common along streams in the Terai and in swampy places in the hills up to 3,000 ft. I have never seen the male tree. Fr. 12-1.

SALIX BABYLONICA, Linn. L. $\frac{30\text{-}40}{10\text{-}15+3\text{-}4}$. Extensively planted in the hills, where it grows very fast, especially in wet places. There are fine trees, both in Darjeeling and Kurseong. Propagated from cuttings.

SALIX (ELEGANS, Wall). Small tree; cultivated about Darjeeling.

POPULUS CILIATA, Wall. *Bangikat, P.*; *Sugribong-kúng, L.* *L.* $\frac{60\text{-}80}{30\text{-}40+4\text{-}6}$ of the M. H. F. and downwards to 1,000 ft. Scarce west of the Tista, but common in the Dumsong forests Bark smooth when young; when old, rough with deep vertical fissures. Wood said to be good for planking, but rarely used. In the Sivoke Hills very large specimens may be seen. Fl. fr. 3.

CONIFERÆ.

PINUS LONGIFOLIA, Roxb. *Dhup*; *Neet-kúng, L.* E. $\frac{50\text{-}60}{10\text{-}20+3\text{-}4}$. Only found in dry southern slopes in the inner ranges between 1,000 and 3,000 ft., where the rainfall is comparatively small. There is only one small forest in British territory, viz. Badamtam, between the Rungnoo and Great Rangít rivers, but a few isolated trees also occur in the Reyang forest. On the north side of the Great Rangít and Tista rivers, in the Raja of Sikkim's territory, it forms large forests, which will probably prove valuable hereafter, though at present there is little or no demand for the wood.

Fl. 3, fr. 4-5 (after one year). Wood formerly used in Darjeeling for planking and shingles, but its use has for a long time been discontinued. Its quality is very variable; generally it is soft and rots easily, but some specimens which I have seen in Julpiguri in carpenters' shops have been strong and full of resin. In the forest it is almost always mixed with sâl.

PINUS EXCELSA, Wall. This tree is only found planted in Darjeeling for ornament, but it is indigenous to Nepal and Bhutan, and perhaps to Sikkim. It is being grown in the Rungbool nurseries from seed obtained from the North-Western Provinces, and the young seedlings have thriven well so far.

CEDRUS DEODARA, Loudon. E. Planted in Darjeeling for ornament, but not indigenous, though it is said to have been found in Bhutan by Griffith. It does not thrive well, though a few fine young specimens are to be seen in different gardens. The cause of its failure is, no doubt, due to the heavy rainfall, and to the unsuitability of the clayey soil. Large numbers are being reared in the Rungbool nurseries in prepared beds, and they are doing well so far.

ABIES WEBBIANA, Ldl. *Dumshing, Bh.* E. The Indian silver fir. E. $\frac{40\text{-}60}{20\text{-}30+6\text{-}10}$ above 10,000 feet on the Singalila range. On the tops of the ridges is found generally in scattered clumps; but where it has tolerable shelter, as on the Phallalúng spur below Suburkum, it forms dense forest, the trees being very fine, with well-grown straight stems. Its natural reproduction is very good, but the seedlings on the ridges have much difficulty in growing, owing to their being constantly eaten down by sheep. Fine patches of young forest may be seen on Sundukpho, to the east of the summit. On the ridges the number of dry dead trees is very remarkable, the stems having become bleached by the wet and the sun. These have died partly naturally, partly by fires burning the touchwood of the centre of the stem, which has rotted from age; partly by being killed by having the bark cut off by Nepalese and Bhutia graziers to make cattle troughs. The whole of the forests lie on the lands of Cheeboo Lama, whose agent has lately introduced strict rules for their protection. The wood is little used, as the forests are so difficult of access; but it is a very good deal, and would be valuable were it possible to bring it into the station. It splits easily, and is used by the Bhutias for shingles, and has occasionally been brought to Darjeeling for that purpose—one house, at least, in the station being roofed with them. It has been grown in Darjeeling for ornament, and appears to succeed well and to be worthy of more extensive introduction.

ABIES SMITHIANA, Forbes. E. *Sehshing, Bh.* The Indian spruce. Not found wild within the limits of the district, but is common in Independent Sikkim. Has been introduced into Darjeeling, where a few fine specimens may be seen. It appears to grow quickly.

Abies dumosa, Loudon. *Tangshing, Bh.* The Indian hemlock. E. $\frac{60\text{-}80}{10\text{-}20+10\text{-}15}$. Forms forests in the inner ranges from 8,000 to 10,000 feet below the *A. Webbiana.* The undergrowth in these forests is chiefly small bamboo with rhododendrons and laurels. The wood is said to be rather better than that of *A. Webbiana*, and is used for similar purposes. Old trees are not, however, so liable to get hollow. The best forests of this tree in the district are in the Siri valley. It has been much planted in Darjeeling.

Larix Griffithii, Hk. f. and T. L. The larch is not indigenous to the district, but is found in the adjoiuing territories of Nepal, Sikkim, and Bhutan. It has not yet been successfully introduced.

Cupressus funebris, Endl. E. *Chandang, Bh.* Planted near monasteries in Sikkim and Bhutan, and extensively in the station of Darjeeling, where it thrives well. It has been grown by the Forest Department in plantation at Dhobi Jhora, near Kurseong, and seems to have succeeded well. A fine big tree may be seen at the Tasingthong Monastery near Dumsong.

Cryptomeria Japonica, Don. E. This handsome tree is now being extensively grown in the district, where it thrives wonderfully. It grows best at an altitude of 3,000 to 5,000 ft., as may be seen from the fine specimens at Soom, Poomong, and elsewhere: but there are also several very fine specimens in Darjeeling. It grows very quickly, often reaching 6 to 8 ft. in height in two years. It is one of the trees planted at Dhobi Jhora plantation, and plants are also being reared in quantity at Rungbool and Rungyrúm. I have not seen the wood, but I have been assured by several gentlemen who have tried it that it is rather soft, but close-grained and easily worked; that for boxes it is exceedingly good; and that it has no resinous smell, like most of the *coniferæ*.

Thuja orientalis, L. E. One of the trees grown in the Dhobi Jhora plantation, also planted about the station of Darjeeling.

Juniperus recurva, Ham. E. *Chukboo, L.* E. $\frac{20\text{-}30}{0\text{-}15+2\text{-}3}$ from 9,000 to 12,000 ft. It is not uncommon about Sundukpho, but it is chiefly found in Sikkim, whence the twigs and leaves are much exported to burn in temples as incense. Bark red-brown, papery, peeling off in vertical strips. Sapwood white, inconsiderable; wood reddish brown, very fragrant, but not much used. Countings on a section of 9 in. mean diameter gave 164 years of age and a mean annual increment ·027 in., thus it is very slow growing.

Podocarpus neriifolia, Don. A small tree of the evergreen forests on the northern slopes of the outer hills. Common in the Sivoke Hills—from the valley to 2,000 ft. Wood said to be hard and close-grained.

Taxus baccata, L. *Tsa, Bh.*; *Cheongboo, L.* E. $\frac{40\text{-}70}{10\text{-}30+10\text{-}20}$. Found only on the upper ranges from 8,000 to 10,000. Many fine specimens may be seen on the path from Tongloo to Kinjalia. The measurements of two were:—

No. 1.—L. 30 ft., G. 20 ft., length to first branch 10 ft.

No. 2.—L. 70 ft., G. 16 ft., length to first branch 30 ft.

Many other *coniferæ* have also been introduced and planted in the hills, such as *Pinus Khasya*, Royle; *Juniperus Sabina*; *Cupressus torulosa*, Don; and species of *Podocarpus*, *Thuja*, and *Araucaria*.

CYCADACEÆ.

CYCAS PECTINATA, Griff. E. $\frac{10\text{-}15}{4\text{-}8+1\text{-}3}$. Common in the lower sâl forests of the Terai, such us the Sath Bhaia and Tehsilpur Jhars, also in dry sâl forests of the Lower Hills and the valleys, *e.g.* at Chenga and Pashok. Fl. 11-12, fr. 12-1. Wood very curious, soft, arranged in concentric rings, separated by white tissue, which, like the central pith, is full of starc hy granules.

PALMÆ.

ARECA CATECHU, Linn. *Supari*. Cultivated in the lower part of the Terai, and about Julpiguri. A few well-grown ones may be seen at Garidura, below Pankabari.

ARECA GRACILIS, Roxb. *Khur, L.* E. $\frac{10\text{-}15}{8\text{-}12+\frac{1}{2}\text{-}\frac{3}{4}}$. Common in the M. P. F. *w.* of Terai and valleys of L. H. F. up to 2,000 ft.

WALLICHIA DENSIFLORA, Mart. *Ooh, L.*; *Takoru, P.* E. 2-10, with no clear stem. Very common in L. and M. H. F. up to 4,000 ft., especially on rocks under dense forest. Leaves very good for feeding ponies. The midrib of the leaves is used by Paharias to make combs.

WALLICHIA DISTICHA, T. And. *Katong, L.* E. $\frac{15\text{-}20}{5\text{-}10+1\text{-}1\frac{1}{2}}$ with distichous leaves joined together at their base by shaggy fibres, which are strong, though not economically used. Wood soft, except a thin (⅓ in.) circle on the outside, which is hard, brown, with scattered black vascular bundles. The Lepchas eat the pith near the summit of the tree; and as they have to cut it down for that purpose, big ones are gradually getting rare. It is very common in the Sivoke Hills up to 2,000 ft. from the plains to the Ruyem river, and all along as far as the Cart Road, west of which I have never seen it.

CARYOTA URENS, L. *Rungbong, P.*; *Simong, L.* E. $\frac{30\text{-}40}{20\text{-}30+2\text{-}3}$, with much divided leaves and cuneate leaflets. Wood, outer part very hard, heavy, with broad, black, closely-grown vascular bundles, and easily worked without splitting; inner part soft, with a sago-giving pith. The Lepchas eat this green, but I have never heard of sago being ever extracted by them. It is rare as a big tree in consequence of its being cut down by Lepchas, and I once saw in a small stream running into the Panchenai river

(Chibla Khola) no less than three big ones of about 20 feet in height freshly cut, but small ones are common in all the L. H. F. and occasionally up to 4,000 ft.

CALAMUS SCHIZOSPATHUS, Griff. *Rong, L.* E. $\frac{30\text{-}40}{10\text{-}20+\frac{1}{2}\text{-}\frac{3}{4}}$. Erect growing, the commonest cane in the L. H. forests and up to 3,000 ft. The canes are useless.

CALAMUS FLAGELLUM, Griff. *Rabi Bet, P.*; *Reem, L.* E. climber common in M. P. F. *w.* (Dalka Jhar and Singari Puhar forests especially) and L. H. F. up to 3,000 ft. Canes soft, only used for tying. Leaves resemble those of the preceding, but differ in that the thorns of *C. schizospathus* are in horizontal semicircular whorls on the rachis, while these of *L. flagellum* are vertically arranged, and alternately long and short.

CALAMUS LEPTOSPADIX, Griff. *Dangri Bet, P.*; *Lat, L.* E. climbing, common in the valleys of the L. H. F., especially in very damp places along rivers, where it forms a tangled thicket. The canes are thin and useless. Recognized easily by its narrow feathery foliage, which is very pretty.

CALAMUS MONTANUS, T. And. *Gouri Bet, P.*; *Rue, L.* E. climber of about 3,000 to 6,000 ft. The best species of cane in the district, but very rare now west of the Tista. In the Chel and Neora valleys east of the Tista it forms dense thickets mixed with *Plectocomia*. I have also seen a few above Pomong and Hoom-Linding, and seedlings may constantly be met with, though after about 6 ft. in height they are eagerly sought for to make walking-sticks. This is the cane which is chiefly employed in the construction of bridges, and it is the best for chair-making.

CALAMUS MACRACANTHUS, T. And. *Paekori Bet, P.*; *Ruebee, L.* E. climber of the M. P. F. *w.* of Terai (Singari Puhar near Sivoke) and L. H. F. Canes thick, long, strong; but as they are not very common, rarely used. Easily recognized by its broad leaflets and green-coloured stems, which lose their lower leaves quickly.

CALAMUS INERMIS, T. And. *Dangri Bet, P.*; *Brool, L.* Climber, good for most purposes, but chiefly cut to make the big thick alpenstock walking-sticks sold in Darjeeling. I have never seen this cane, but mention it as it is often spoken of by Lepchas and described by Dr. Anderson, from whose account in the Journal of the Linnean Society (Palms of Sikkim) the names of the different canes here mentioned are obtained. It is now rare, and collectors cannot always find specimens.

CALAMUS (ROTANG, Willd.). *Bet, Bg.* Climber; only found in marshy places in the southern Terai south of the big sâl forests. Found by me at the edge of the Sath Bhaia Jhar. Common on the roadside between Titalya and Kishenganj, and in the Western Duars.

CYMBOSPATHES JENKINSIANUS, Griff. E. climber. The commonest species in the Terai M. P. F. *w.*, but only seen by me in two forests, viz. the Dalka Jhar and Singari Puhar M. P. F. near Sivoke. Canes very long, rather soft, used to make baskets.

PLECTOCOMIA HIMALAYANA, Griff. *Takri Bet, P.*; *Runool, L.* E. climber of the M. and U. H. F. from 4,000 to 7,000 ft. Exceedingly common. Canes soft; useless, except sometimes for tying fences and for rough baskets.

LIVISTONA JENKINSIANA, Griff. *Talainyom, L.*; *Purbong, L.* E. $\frac{20\text{-}30}{15\text{-}25+2\text{-}3}$ of the L. H. F. between the Tista river and the Cart Road. The only fan-palm of the district except *Licuala peltata*, which is said to have been once found. Big specimens are scarce, but may still be seen in the forests at the back of the big precipice above Sivoke. Young trees, about 6 to 10 ft. high, are not uncommon in the valleys of the Tista and Mahanadi. Wood very soft, useless. Leaves often 3 feet in diameter; used by Lepchas to thatch their houses, for which purpose they are very good. They may also be seen used as umbrellas.

COCOS NUCIFERA, L. A few specimens of the cocoanut may be seen planted near villages in Terai. There is a good sized one behind the thana at Nuxelbari.

PHŒNIX ACAULIS, Roxb. E., stemless, with a large bulbous-looking rootstock, occasionally reaching 2 to 3 ft. in height in the lower Terai Very common in the sâl forests of the Tista and Great Rangít valleys, *e.g.* Badamtam and Pashok. Occasionally found in the sâl forests of the Terai, *e.g.* Sivoke, also in the open grass lands of the southern Terai and Duars. Fruit eaten by Lepchas.

PHŒNIX RUPICOLA, T. And. *Schiap, L.* E. $\frac{15\text{-}20}{13\text{-}18+1\frac{1}{2}\text{-}3}$ of the L. H. F. of the Tista and Mahanadi valleys; not seen west of the latter river. It generally grows on rocks, and especially on the very steep cliffs on both sides of the Tista above Sivoke. The interior of the stem is eaten by Lepchas, but without cooking.

PANDANEÆ.

PANDANUS (FURCATUS, Roxb.). *Bor-kûng, L.* E. $\frac{20\text{-}30}{10\text{-}15+\frac{1}{2}\text{-}1}$ with numerous thick soft aërial roots from the lower part of the stem. Found common all over the L. H. F. up to 3,000 ft. Outer wood hard, with satiny white vascular bundles, closely set; inner wood soft, useless.

PANDANUS (FŒTIDUS, Roxb.). E. shrub with densely matted stems and roots. Common in M. P. F. *w.*, as in the Dalka Jhar.

NOTE.—Two or three species of *Musa*, or wild plantain, are common throughout the district up to 6,000 ft. elevation; and one of the *Scitamineæ*, *Alpinia nutans*, Roscoe, forms a dense growth, rising to 10 or 15 ft. high in damp swampy places in the Terai They are all much used as elephant fodder. Some of the species of *Smilax* grow into woody-stemmed climbers.

GRAMINEÆ.

ARUNDINARIA (FALCATA, Nees). *Titi nigala, P.*; *Prongnok, L.* Small thin bamboo with cæspitose, generally annual stems. Nodes swollen. Sheath long, thin, glabrous. Found in the

M. H. F. about 5,000 to 6,000 ft. Used for many small purposes, such as mats, baskets, house-tying, &c.

THAMNOCALAMUS (SPATHIFLORUS, Munro). *Prong, L.*; *Begoha, Bh.* A small bamboo with cœspitose stems. The halm is yellow, hard, and the branches red, with long thin sheaths. Common on the Singalila ridge from Tongloo 10,000 ft. up.

THAMNOCALAMUS (FALCONERI, Hk. f.). *Maling, P.*; *Phyeum, L.* The commonest of the small hill bamboos. Found everywhere in the U. H. F. from 5,000 to 9,000 ft. Used for hedges in Darjeeling. Grows 15 to 20 ft. high. Leaves in semi-whorls; very dense and close. Halms as well as sheaths roughly pubescent. Used to make mats for roofing and for floors, to tie houses, &c. The leaves are the chief food for ponies in Darjeeling.

(THAMNOCALAMUS, SP). *Kasre-maling, P.*; *Phyeum, L.* Resembles the preceding, but the leaves not in such dense whorls. Found in U. H. F., and used for the same purposes as *Maling.*

BAMBUSA (BALCOOA, Roxb.). *Bleeng, L.* The large village bamboo of the Bengali villages in the Terai. Yellowish, halms strong, with only a slight hollow in the middle. Grows to a great height. Used for every purpose in the Terai, and is the best for house-building, but should be seasoned in water before use.

BAMBUSA NUTANS, Wall. *Mahlbans, P.*; *Mahlu, L.* A large graceful bamboo of the L. and M. H F. from 1,000 to 5,000 ft. Not very common. The halm is of large diameter, with a broad hollow part, but the wood is hard.

DENDROCALAMUS HAMILTONII, Nees et Arnott. *Pao, L.* The common forest bamboo of the L. H. F. up to 3,000 ft. Covers large tracts in the lower hills, and especially in the Tista valley, where it grows in sâl forests to the great damage of the sâl. It often reaches 6 to 8 inches in diameter, and the halms have very thick walls when old. It grows very straight to 40 or 50 ft. occasionally. It is used for all purposes, for water-vessels, house-building, fences, mats, baskets, &c. It is used by the Department to float heavy logs. Its young shoots, which appear in June, are eaten, and make a very good vegetable.

Filing, P.; *Paphok, L.* A middle-sized bamboo of the L. and M. H. F. up to 4,000 ft. Common in the damp forests of the Lower Hills. The halms are soft, with thin walls. They are preferred for tying houses, and are among the best for baskets and mats, especially those used in tea factories.

Singhani, P.; *Pagjiokpo, L.* A medium-sized cœspitose bamboo, with glaucous stems, of the L. and M. H. F. from about 2,000 to 5,000 ft. Not very common. Fine clumps of it may be seen planted in the Bhutia Busti at Darjeeling.

CEPHALOSTACHYUM CAPITATUM, Munro. *Gobia, P.*; *Payong, L.* A very common medium-sized bamboo of the L. M. and U. H. F.

from 2,000 to 6,000 ft. It is new (1877), only just coming up afresh as it flowered and died off in 1874. The halms are yellow coloured, strong, and hard, and are preferred by the Lepchas for making bows and arrows. The leaves are excellent fodder. In some places, such as in the valleys of the Chel and Neora, it covered in 1874 large tracts of country almost alone.

NOTE.—There are several other kinds, for instance *Pugriang*, L., a very large bamboo of the Hills, at about an elevation of 3,000 to 4,000 ft.; but many of them are very likely not yet named, owing to the difficulty in obtaining flowers. During a residence of nearly five years in the district, I have only obtained flowers of two kinds, one of which, *Dendrocalamus Hamiltonii*, flowers almost yearly. Some of the grasses of the Terai and Lower Hills, such as *Arundo saccharum*, &c., grow very large, and are used for many purposes,—thatch, fodder, mats, baskets, &c.

FILICES.

ALSOPHILA LATEBROSA, Hk. *Unyo, Pakpa, P.*; *Pashien, L.* E. $\frac{20\text{-}30}{15\text{-}20+2\text{-}3}$ of the M. H. F. from 4,000 to 6,000 ft. This is the common kind of tree fern seen round Darjeeling. The Lepchas eat the soft part of the interior of the stem.

ALSOPHILA CONTAMINANS, Wall. *Pakjik, L.* E. $\frac{10\text{-}20}{5\text{-}15+2\text{-}3}$ of the L. H. F. up to 4,000 ft. Recognized by the leaves being glaucous beneath.

ALSOPHILA SCOTTIANA, Baker. Tree fern of the M. H. F. Rare. Occasionally branched. Found, I believe, now only in one spot near Rungbi.

ALSOPHILA GLABRA, Hk. E. $\frac{10\text{-}15}{0\text{-}5+1}$ of the M. P. F. *w.* in Terai (common in the Dalka Jhar) and L. H. F. valleys.

HEMITELIA DECIPIENS, Scott. E. $\frac{10\text{-}20}{5\text{-}15+1\text{-}2}$ of the M. H. F. Rare. I have only once seen it, near Kalimpung.

NOTE.—There are several other large-growing ferns, of which should be mentioned *Angiopteris evecta*, Hoffm., and *Diplazium polypodioides*, Mett.; the former common throughout the district in damp ravines, the latter of the U. H. forests.

THE END.

ADDITIONS AND CORRECTIONS.

Page 1, line 16 from below, *for* 'GREWIŒFLORA' *read* 'GREWIÆFLORA.'
,, 4, ,, 10, *for* 'ASPIDO CARYA' *read* 'ASPIDOCARYA.'
,, 5, ,, 4 from below, *for* 'CRATŒVA' *read* 'CRATÆVA.'
,, 7, ,, 7, *for* 'Patulum' *read* 'patulum.'
,, 10, ,, ,, from below, *for* '*Kunhlyem-kúng*' *read* '*Kanhlyem-kúng*.'
,, 14, ,, 9, *for* 'Zalatum' *read* 'Z. alatum.'
,, ,, ,, 23, *for* '*Timbernyok*' *read* '*Timburnyok*.'
,, 16, ,, 17, *for* 'Hook. *f.*' *read* 'Hk. fil.'
,, 17, ,, 18, *for* '*Lapshi*' *read* '*Labshi*.'
,, 21, ,, 19, *for* 'LŒTA' *read* 'LÆTA.'
,, 22, ,, 2, *for* '*Kautiernyok*' *read* '*Kantiernyok*.'
,, 23, ,, 14, *for* 'DOBINŒA' *read* 'DOBINÆA.'
,, ,, ,, 16, *for* 'DODONŒA' *read* 'DODONÆA.'
,, 26, ,, 6 from below, *for* '*Tirhyukmyok*' *read* '*Tirhyuknyok*.'
,, 27, ,, 12 *after* '. . . . . . . rarely used' *add* 'in the Darjeeling district, but which is exported from other parts of India as a medicine under the name of' "kino."
,, 28, lines 22 and 26, *for* '*Debre-lara*' *read* '*Belcri-lara*.'
,, 33, line 10, *for* 'CŒSIA' *read* 'CÆSIA.'
,, 34, ,, 26, *for* 'GASTANOSPERMUM' *read* 'CASTANOSPERMUM.'
,, 35, ,, 11, *for* 'ACUMINATUS' *read* 'ACUMINATA.'
,, ,, ,, 21, *for* 'Lal' *read* 'Ldl.'
,, ,, ,, 28, *after* 'MOLUCCANUS' *read* 'LINN.'
,, ,, ,, ,, *for* '*Sufokji*' *read* '*Siphokji*.'
,, 36, ,, 13 from below, *for* 'lepidotus' *read* 'lepidotum.'
,, 41, ,, 12, *for* 'PRŒCOX' *read* 'PRÆCOX.'
,, 43, ,, 13 from below, *for* 'NOIIOLOSA' *read* 'FOLIOLOSA.'
,, ,, ,, 4 from below, *for* 'in' *read* 'on.'
,, 45, ,, 11, *for* 'BEGONIŒFOLIA' *read* 'BEGONIÆFOLIA.'
,, ,, ,, 10 from below, *for* 'TILIŒFOLIA' *read* '*Tiliæfolia*.'
,, 47, ,, 5, *for* '*Kahuk-rig*' *read* '*Kahuk-rik*.'
,, ,, ,, 29, *for* 'with white bracts' *read* 'with whitish floral leaves.'
,, 48, lines 13 and 17, *for* 'MUSSŒNDA' *read* 'MUSSÆNDA.'
,, ,, line 18 from below, *for* 'PŒDERIA' *read* 'PÆDERIA.'
,, 52, lines 2 and 3 from below, *for* '*Monkyou-rig*' *read* '*Monkyou-rik*.'
,, 53, line 23, *for* '$\frac{5-10}{0-5+\frac{1}{2}}$' *read* '$\frac{5-10}{0-5+\frac{1}{2}-1}$.'
,, 54, ,, 14 from below, *for* '*Timbernyok*' *read* '*Timburnyok*.'
,, 56, ,, 8 from below, *after* 'COLVILLEI' *read* 'Hk. f. and T.'
,, ,, ,, 3 from below, *for* 'FAGREA' *read* 'FAGRÆA.'
,, 57, ,, 4, *for* 'LŒVIS' read 'LÆVIS.'
,, 59, lines 31 and 34, *for* 'DŒDALACANTHUS' *read* 'DÆDALACANTHUS.'
,, 61, line 17, *for* '*Monkakrig*' *read* '*Monkakrik*.'
,, 63, ,, ,, from below, *for* '*Nupsorgkúng*' *read* '*Nupsorkúng*.'
,, ,, ,, 3 from below, *after* 'CAUDATUM' *read* 'Nees.'
,, 65, ,, 4 from below, *for* '*Tirhilzok-kúng*' *read* '*Terhilzok-kúng*.'
,, 68, ,, 1, *omit the word* 'perhaps.'
,, ,, ,, 9, *after* 'THOMSONI' *add* 'Müll. Arg.'
,, 69, ,, 20, *for* '*Kautjer*' *read* '*Kantjer*.'

Page 70, line 7, *for* '*Takchabrig*' *read* '*Takchabrik.*'
,, 71, ,, 6 from below, *after* '*Jagrikat*' *read* '*Bajadanti.*'
,, 72, ,, 13, *for* 'EXCÆCARIA' *read* 'EXCŒCARIA.'
,, ,, *after* line 18, *add* 'EXCŒCARIA SEBIFERA, Müll. Arg., the "Tallow Tree," is often found planted for ornament in the Terai and lower hills.'
,, 75, line 8, *for* '*Kungji-kúng*' *read* '*Kangji-kúng.*'
,, 78, *to the description of* '*Quercus lamellosa,*' *add* 'Acorns very large, the cups often two to three inches in diameter, and composed of broad annular rings: in some years extremely abundant, in others very scarce.'
,, ,, *to the description of* '*Quercus annulata,*' *add* 'Acorns small; the cups shallow, surrounded by small thin annular rings.'
,, ,, *to the description of* '*Quercus spicata,*' *add* 'Acorns rather flattened, on shallow scaly cups, several together on a long upright spike.'
,, 79, line 4, *for* 'fruit' *substitute* 'Acorns large, deeply bedded in scaly cups,'
,, 88, *for* 'saccharum' *read* 'Saccharum.'

INDEX OF ORDERS, GENERA, AND SPECIES.

PAGE.

A.

Abies dumosa 83
„ Smithiana 82
„ Webbiana 82
Abroma augusta 11
Abrus precatorius 27
„ pulchellus 27
Abutilon 10
Acacia cæsia 33
„ Catechu 32
„ concinna 33
„ ferruginea 32
„ pennata 33
ACANTHACEÆ 59
Acer Campbellii 23
„ caudatum 22
„ Hookeri 22
„ lævigatum 22
„ oblongum 22
„ Sikkimense 22
„ Thomsoni 22
Acrocarpus fraxinifolius 30
Acronychia laurifolia 14
Actinidia callosa 8
„ strigosa 8
Actinodaphne obovatum 65
Adenosacme longifolia 48
Adhatoda Vasica 60
Adina cordifolia 46
Æchmanthera Wallichii 60
Ægle marmelos 15
Aerva scandens 63
Æsculus Punduana 22
Aganosma 55
Agapetes saligna 50
Aglaia edulis 16
Albizzia Julibrissin 34
„ Lebbek 33
„ lucida 33
„ odoratissima 33
„ procera 33
„ stipulata 34
Alchornea tiliæfolia 71
Allamanda cathartica 56
Allophylus Zeylanicus 23
Alnus Nepalensis 80
Alpinia nutans 86
Alsodeia Bengalensis 6
Alsophila contaminans 88
„ glabra 88
„ latebrosa 88
„ Scottiana 88
Alstonia scholaris 55
„ venenata 55
AMARANTACEÆ 63
Amoora decandra 16
„ Rohituka 16
AMPELIDEÆ 19
ANACARDIACEÆ 24
Andromeda ovalifolia 50
Angiopteris evecta 88

PAGE.

ANONACEÆ 3
Anona squamosa 3
Anthocephalus Cadamba 46
Antidesma Bunias 69
„ diandrum 69
„ Menasu 69
Aperula Neesiana 65
APOCYNEÆ 55
Aporosa dioica 69
„ Lindleyana 69
ARALIACEÆ 43
Aralia foliolosa 43
Araucaria 84
Ardisia crenulata 53
„ floribunda 53
„ humilis 53
„ involucrata 53
„ macrocarpa 53
Areca Catechu 84
„ gracilis 84
Argyreia capitata 57
„ pomacea 57
„ setosa 57
„ speciosa 57
ARISTOLOCHIACEÆ 67
Aristolochia Roxburghiana 67
„ saccata 67
Artemisia vulgaris 50
Artocarpus chaplasha 73
„ integrifolia 73
„ Lakoocha 73
Arundinaria falcata 86
Arundo 88
ASCLEPIADACEÆ 56
Aspidocarya uvifera 4
Aspidopterys nutans 13
„ Roxburghiana 13
Aucuba Himalaica 45
Averrhoa Carambola 13

B.

Baccaurea sapida 69
Bambusa Balcooa 87
„ nutans 87
Barleria cœrulea 59
„ cristata 59
Barringtonia acutangula 41
Bassia butyracea 53
Bauhinia anguina 31
„ macrophylla 31
„ Malabarica 31
„ purpurea 31
„ Vahlii 31
„ variegata 31
Beaumontia grandiflora 56
Beilschmiedia Roxburghiana 64
BERBERIDEÆ 4
Berberis angulosa 5
„ aristata 5

PAGE.

Berberis concinna 5
„ insignis 5
„ Nepalensis 5
„ umbellata 5
Berchemia floribunda 19
Betula acuminata 79
„ Bhojpattra 79
„ cylindrostachys 80
BIGNONIACEÆ 68
Bischoffia Javanica 69
Bixa Orellana 6
BIXINEÆ 6
Böhmeria Hamiltoniana 76
„ macrophylla 76
„ Malabarica 76
„ platyphylla 76
„ polystachya 76
„ rugulosa 76
BORAGINEÆ 57
Bombax malabaricum 10
Brassaiopsis floribunda 44
„ hispida 44
Briedelia montana 70
„ retusa 69
„ stipularis 69
„ tomentosa 70
Brucea mollis 16
Bucklandia populnea 88
Buddleia Asiatica 56
„ Colvillei 56
„ paniculata 56
BURSERACEÆ 15
Butea frondosa 27
„ minor 27
Byttneria aspera 12
„ pilosa 11

C.

Cæsalpinia Bonducella 30
Cæsalpinieæ 30
Calamus flagellum 85
„ inermis 85
„ leptospadix 85
„ macracanthus 85
„ montanus 85
„ rotang 85
„ schizospathus 85
Callicarpa arborea 60
„ cana 60
„ lanata 60
„ rubella 60
Calophyllum polyanthum . . . 7
Calosanthes Indica 59
Calotropis gigantea 56
Camellia drupifera 9
„ thea 9
„ theifera 9
Canarium Bengalense 15
CAPPARIDEÆ 5
Capparis floribunda 5
„ multiflora 5
„ olacifolia 5
„ pumila 5
„ viminea 5
CAPRIFOLIACEÆ 46
Carallia integerrima 39
Careya arborea 41
„ herbacea 41
Carica Papaya 43
Caryopteris Wallichiana 62
Caryota urens 84

PAGE.

Casearia glomerata 42
„ Hamiltonii 43
„ Vareca 43
Cassia Fistula 30
„ obovata 31
„ occidentalis 31
Castanopsis argentea 79
„ Indica 79
„ rufescens 79
„ tribuloides 79
Castanospermum Australe . . . 34
Cedrela toona 16
Cedrus deodara 82
CELASTRINEÆ 18
Celastrus monosperma 19
„ paniculata 18
„ stylosa 19
Celtis tetrandra 72
„ trinervia 72
Cephalostachyum capitatum . . 87
Chasalia curviflora 49
Chonemorpha macrophylla . . . 56
Choripetalum undulatum . . . 63
Cinchona Calisaya 47
„ micrantha 47
„ officinalis 47
„ succirubra 47
Cinnamomum caudatum 63
„ glanduliferum . . . 64
„ impressinervium . . 64
„ obtusifolium . . . 63
„ Tamala 63
Cissampelos Pareira 4
Citrus Aurantium 15
„ decumana 15
„ medica 15
Clausena excavata 14
„ Willdenovii 15
Cleidion Javanicum 70
Clematis acuminata 1
„ Buchananiana 1
„ grewiæflora 1
„ Gouriana 1
„ montana 1
„ smilacifolia 1
Clerodendron bracteatum . . . 62
„ Colebrookianum . . 62
„ dentatum . . . 62
„ gratum . . . 62
„ infortunatum . . . 62
„ nutans . . . 62
„ serratum . . . 61
„ Siphonanthus . . . 62
„ urticæfolium . . . 62
Cocos nucifera 86
Coffea Arabica 49
„ Bengalensis 49
Colebrookia oppositifolia . . . 63
Colquhounia 63
COMBRETACEÆ 39
Combretum decandrum 40
„ sarcopterum . . . 40
„ squamosum . . . 40
COMPOSITÆ 50
CONIFERÆ 81
Conocephalus suaveolens . . . 77
CONVOLVULACEÆ 57
Conyza balsamifera 50
Cordia grandis 57
„ Myxa 57
CORNACEÆ 45
Cornus capitata 45

PAGE.

Cornus macrophylla 45
Corylus ferox 79
Cotoneaster microphylla . . . 87
Cratœgus Oxyacantha 87
Cratæva religiosa 5
Crotalaria juncea 25
" sericea 25
" striata 25
" tetragona 25
Croton caudatus 70
" oblongifolius 70
" polyandrus 70
Cryptocarya amygdalina . . . 64
" floribunda 64
Cryptomeria Japonica 83
Cudrania Javanensis 73
Cupressus funebris 83
" torulosa 84
CUPULIFERÆ 78
CYCADACEÆ 84
Cycas pectinata 84
Cyclostemon subsessile . . . 69
Cymbospathes Jenkinsianus . . 85
Cytisus Laburnum 84

D.

Dædalacanthus nervosus . . . 59
" splendens . . . 59
Dalbergia foliacea 29
" hircina 30
" lanceolaria 29
" latifolia 29
" Sissoo 28
" stenocarpa 29
" stipulacea 29
" tamarindifolia 29
Daphne longifolia 67
" papyracea 67
" Wallichii 67
Daphnidium elongatum . . . 65
" pulcherrimum . . . 65
Daphniphyllopsis capitata . . . 18
DATISCEÆ 43
Debregeasia longifolia 77
Deeringia baccata 63
Delima sarmentosa 2
Dendrocalamus Hamiltonii . . 87
Derris cuneifolia 30
Desmodium Cephalotes 26
" confertum 26
" floribundum 26
" gyrans 26
" gyroides 27
" latifolium 26
" polycarpum 26
" pulchellum 26
Dicellostyles jujubifolia . . . 10
DILLENIACEÆ 1
Dillenia India 1
" pentagyna 2
Diospyros Embryopteris . . . 53
Diplazium polypodioides . . . 88
DIPTEROCARPEÆ 9
Dobinæa vulgaris 23
Dodonæa viscosa 23
Drimycarpus racemosus . . . 25
Duabanga sonneratoides . . . 42
Dysoxylum alliaceum 16
" binectariferum . . . 16
" Hamiltonii 16

E. PAGE.

EBENACEÆ 53
Echinocarpus dasycarpus . . . 12
" sterculiaceus . . . 12
" tomentosus . . . 12
Edgeworthia Gardneri . . . 67
Ehretia lævis 57
" serrata 57
" Wallichiana 57
ELÆAGNACEÆ 67
Elæagnus latifolia 67
Elæocarpus robustus 13
" rugosus 13
" lanceæfolius . . . 13
Embelia floribunda 53
" Ribes 53
" robusta 53
Elæodendron Roxburghii . . . 19
Engelhardtia spicata 81
Enkianthus Himalaicus . . . 50
Entada scandens 32
ERICACEÆ 50
Eriobotrya macrocarpa . . . 38
Eriolæna 11
Erythrina arborescens . . . 27
" stricta 27
" suberosa 27
Erythropalum scandens . . . 18
Eucalyptus globulus 41
Eugenia balsamea 41
" caryophyllæfolia . . . 40
" cerasiflora 41
" claviflora 41
" formosa 40
" Jambolana 40
" Jambos 40
" lanceæfolia 40
" obovata 40
" præcox 41
" ramosissima 40
" toddaliæfolia 41
EUPHORBIACEÆ 68
Euphorbia neriifolia 72
" pulcherrima 72
Eurya acuminata 7
" Japonica 7
" symplocina 7
Evodia fraxinifolia 13
Evonymus echinatus 18
" frigidus 18
" theæfolius 18
Excœcaria baccata 72
" sebifera ii

F.

Fagræa obovata 56
Feronia Elephantum 15
Ficus altissima 74
" Bengalensis 73
" Chittagonga 76
" clavata 75
" comosa 74
" cordifolia 75
" Cunia 76
" cyrtophylla 75
" elastica 74
" foveolata 75
" gemella 75
" glomerata 76
" hispida 76
" infectoria 75
" laccifera 74

PAGE.

Ficus macrophylla 75
„ monticola 75
„ Mysorensis 73
„ obtusifolia 74
„ pisifera 75
„ pyriformis 76
„ regia 76
„ religiosa 75
„ retusa 75
„ Roxburghii 75
„ scandens 75
„ Thomsoni 74
FILICES 88
Flemingia involucrata 28
„ semialata 28
„ stricta 28
„ strobilifera 28
Fraxinus floribunda 55

G.

Garcinia pedunculata 7
„ stipulata 7
Gardneria ovata 57
Garuga pinnata 15
Gaultheria Griffithiana 51
„ repens 51
GERANIACEÆ 13
GESNERACEÆ 58
Gironniera Thomsoni 73
Glochidion 68
Glycosmis pentaphylla 14
Gmelina arborea 61
Goniothalamus sesquipedalis . . . 3
Gouania leptostachya 19
GRAMINEÆ 86
Grewia excelsa 12
„ lævigata 12
„ multiflora 12
„ polygama 12
„ sapida 12
„ scabrophylla 12
„ vestita 12
GUTTIFERÆ 7
Gymnema tingens 56
Gymnosporia Thomsoni 19
Gynocardia odorata 6

H.

HAMAMELIDEÆ 38
Hamiltonia suaveolens 49
Hedera Helix 45
Hedyotis capitellata 48
Helicia Cochin-Chinensis 66
„ robusta 66
Helwingia Himalaica 44
Hemitelia decipiens 88
Henslowia heterantha 67
Heptapleurum elatum 44
„ glaucum 44
„ tomentosum 44
„ venulosum 44
Heteropanax fragrans 44
Heynea trijuga 16
Hibiscus scandens 10
Hiptage Madablota 13
Holarrhena antidysenterica . . . 55
Hollböllia latifolia 6
Holmskioldia sanguinea 62
Homonoya riparia 71
„ symphylliæfolia . . . 71

PAGE.

Hydrangea altissima 38
„ robusta 38
„ vestita 38
Hymenodictyon flaccidum . . . 47
„ thyrsiflorum . . . 47
Hymenopogon parasiticus . . . 47
HYPERICINEÆ 6
Hypericum Hookerianum . . . 6
„ patulum 7

I.

Ichnocarpus fragrans 55
Ilex dipyrena 18
„ Godayam 18
„ insignis 18
ILICINEÆ 19
Indigofera cœrulea 26
„ pulchella 25
„ stachyodes 25
Inula Cappa 50
„ eupatorioides 50
Ipomœa atropurpurea 57
„ coccinea 58
Itea macrophylla 38
Ixora acuminata 48
„ coccinea 48
„ tomentosa 48
„ undulata 48

J.

Jasminum dispermum 54
„ grandiflorum 54
„ laurifolium 55
„ pubescens 55
Jatropha Curcas 71
JUGLANDACEÆ 80
Juglans regia 80
Juniperus recurva 83
„ Sabina 84
Justicia gendarussa 60

K.

Kydia calycina 10

L.

LABIATÆ 62
Lagerströmia parviflora 42
Laportea crenulata 77
Larix Griffithii 83
Lasianthus lucidus 49
LAURACEÆ 63
Lawsonia alba 42
Leea alata 21
„ aspera 21
„ crispa 21
„ gigantea 21
„ hirta 21
„ læta 21
„ macrophylla 21
„ robusta 21
„ sambucina 21
„ Sumatrana 21
LEGUMINOSÆ 25
Lepionurus oblongifolius . . . 18
Leptobœa multiflora 58
Leycesteria formosa 46
Licuala peltata 86
Ligustrum robustum 54

	Page.
LINEÆ	13
Litsæa consimilis	65
Livistona Jenkinsiana	86
LOGANIACEÆ	56
Lonicera glabrata	45
" gracilis	46
" Japonica	46
LORANTHACEÆ	66
Loranthus farinosus	66
" globosus	66
" graciliflorus	66
" longiflorus	66
" pentandrus	66
" pentapetalus	66
" viridiflorus	66
Luculia gratissima	47
LYTHRACEÆ	42

M.

Macaranga denticulata	71
" gummiflua	71
" Indica	71
Machilus odoratissimus	64
Macropanax undulatum	46
Mæsa Indica	52
" macrophylla	52
" montana	52
MAGNOLIACEÆ	2
Magnolia Campbellii	2
" globosa	2
Mallotus albus	70
" Helferi	70
" oreophilus	70
" Philippinensis	70
" Roxburghianus	70
MALPIGHIACEÆ	13
MALVACEÆ	10
Mangifera Indica	24
" sylvatica	24
Maoutia Puya	77
Marlea begoniæfolia	45
Marsdenia tinctoria	56
Melanthesopsis patens	68
MELASTOMACEÆ	41
Melastoma malabathricum	41
MELIACEÆ	16
Melia Azedarach	16
" composita	16
Meliosma dilleniæfolia	23
" pinnata	23
" simplicifolia	23
" Wallichii	24
MENISPERMACEÆ	4
Mezoneurum cucullatum	30
Michelia Cathcartii	2
" champaca	3
" excelsa	3
" lanuginosa	2
Micromelum pubescens	14
Microtropis discolor	18
Miliusa macrocarpa	3
" Roxburghiana	4
Millettia auriculata	26
" cinerea	26
" monticola	26
" pachycarpa	26
Mimoseæ	32
Mimosa pudica	23
" rubicaulis	39
Morinda bracteata	42
" lanceolata	49

	Page.
Morus Indica	77
" serrata	77
Mucuna imbricata	27
" macrocarpa	28
" pruriens	28
Munronia Wallichii	16
Murraya exotica	14
" Königii	14
Musa	86
Mussænda frondosa	48
" macrophylla	48
MYRISTICACEÆ	67
Myristica corticosa	68
" longifolia	67
MYRSINACEÆ	52
Myrsine semiserrata	52
MYRTACEÆ	40
Myrtus communis	41

N.

Naravelia Zeylanica	1
Natsiatum herpeticum	18
Neillia thyrsiflora	35
Nerium Oleander	56

O.

OCHNACEÆ	15
Ochna pumila	15
Odina Wodier	24
OLACINEÆ	18
OLEACEÆ	54
Olea dioica	54
Ophioxylon serpentinum	55
Osbeckia angustifolia	42
" Chinensis	42
" crinita	41
" Nepalensis	42
" nutans	42
" paniculata	41
" stellata	41
Osmanthus fragrans	54
Ostodes paniculata	72
Oxyspora paniculata	41

P.

Pæderia fœtida	49
PALMÆ	84
PANDANEÆ	86
Pandanus fœtidus	86
" furcatus	86
Papilionaceæ	25
Paraboena sagittata	4
Paramignya monophylla	15
PASSIFLOREÆ	43
Pentapanax Leschenaultii	43
" racemosum	44
" subcordatum	43
Pentapterygium serpens	50
Pentapyxis stipulata	45
Pergularia odoratissima	56
Periploca calophylla	56
Phlogacanthus pubinervis	60
" thyrsiflorus	60
Phœbe attenuata	64
" glaucescens	64
" lanceolata	64
Phœnix acaulis	86
" rupicola	86

	Page.
Photinia dubia	37
" integrifolia	37
Phyllanthus Andersoni	68
" bicolor	68
" Emblica	68
" fagifolius	68
" lanceolarius	68
" multilocularis	68
" Nepalensis	68
" reticulatus	68
" Thomsoni	68
Picrasma Javanica	15
Pinus excelsa	82
" Khasya	84
" longifolia	81
Piptanthus Nepalensis	25
Pithecolobium angulatum	34
" bigeminum	34
Pittosporeæ	6
Pittosporum floribundum	6
Plectocomia Himalayana	86
Plumeria acutifolia	55
Podocarpus neriifolia	83
Poinsettia pulcherrima	72
Polygala arillata	6
Polygaleæ	6
Polygonaceæ	63
Polygonum crispatum	63
" molle	63
Pongamia glabra	30
Populus ciliata	81
Porana grandiflora	58
" paniculata	58
" volubilis	58
Potentilla fruticosa	36
Pouzolzia viminea	77
Premna barbata	61
" herbacea	61
" integrifolia	60
" interrupta	61
" latifolia	61
" mucronata	61
" racemosa	61
" scandens	61
" tomentosa	61
Priotropis cytisoides	25
Proteaceæ	66
Prunus acuminata	35
" ferruginea	35
" communis	36
" cerasus	35
" Armeniaca	35
" Padus	35
" persica	34
" Puddum	34
Psidium Guava	40
Psychotria calophylla	49
" viridiflora	49
Pterospermum acerifolium	11
Pueraria tuberosa	28
" Wallichii	28
Punica granatum	42
Pygeum acuminatum	35
Pyrularia edulis	66
Pyrus aucuparia	37
" communis	36
" cuspidata	37
" foliolosa	37
" Indica	37
" lanata	37
" microphylla	37
" variolosa	36

Q.

	Page.
Quamoclit coccinea	58
Quercus acuminata	78
" annulata	78, ii
" fenestrata	78
" lamellosa	78, ii
" lanceæfolia	79
" pachyphylla	78
" spicata	78, ii

R.

	Page.
Randia dumetorum	48
" latifolia	48
" rigida	48
" uliginosa	48
Ranunculaceæ	1
Raphistemma pulchellum	56
Reevesia	11
Reinwardtia tetragyna	13
" trigyna	13
Rhamneæ	19
Rhamnus Nepalensis	19
" virgatus	19
Rhizophoreæ	39
Rhododendron arboreum	51
" argenteum	51
" barbatum	51
" campanulatum	51
" Campbelliæ	51
" ciliatum	52
" cinnabarinum	51
" Dalhousiæ	52
" Edgarii	52
" Edgeworthii	52
" Falconeri	51
" fulgens	51
" glaucum	52
" Griffithianum	52
" Hodgsoni	57
" lanatum	52
" lepidotum	36, 52
" Maddeni	52
" pendulum	52
" pumilum	52
" Thomsoni	52
" vaccinioides	52
" virgatum	52
" Wightii	52
Rhodomyrtus	41
Rhus acuminata	24
" insignis	24
" semialata	24
Ribes glaciale	38
Ricinus communis	71
Rivea ornata	57
Rosaceæ	34
Rosa sericea	36
Rottlera tinctoria	73
Rubiaceæ	46
Rubia cordifolia	49
Rubus asper	36
" acuminatus	36
" calycinus	36
" flavus	35
" lasiocarpus	36
" lineatus	36
" macilentus	36
" macrocarpus	35
" moluccanus	35
" niveus	35
" paniculatus	36
" pulcherrimus	36

	PAGE.
Rubus Sikkimensis	36
„ Thomsoni	35
RUTACEÆ	13

S.

Sabia leptandra	23
„ paniculata	23
„ parviflora	23
„ limoniacea	23
SABIACEÆ	23
Saccharum	88
SALICACEÆ	81
Salix Babylonica	81
„ elegans	81
„ tetrasperma	81
Samara frondosa	52
Sambucus adnata	46
„ Javanica	46
SAMYDACEÆ	42
SANTALACEÆ	66
SAPINDACEÆ	22
Sapindus attenuatus	22
SAPOTACEÆ	53
Sarcococca saligna	72
Sarothamnus vulgaris	34
Saurauja fasciculata	8
„ Griffithii	8
„ Nepalensis	8
„ punduana	8
„ Roxburghii	8
Sauropus albicans	69
SAXIFRAGACEÆ	38
Schima Wallichii	8
Schizandra elongata	3
„ grandiflora	3
SCITAMINEÆ	86
Scrophularineæ	58
Securinega Leucopyrus	68
„ obovata	68
Semecarpus Anacardium	25
Sesbania Ægyptiaca	26
Shorea robusta	9
Sideroxylon arboreum	53
„ attenuatum	53
SIMARUBEÆ	15
Skimmia Laureola	14
Smilax	86
SOLANEÆ	58
Solanum crassipetalum	58
„ Indicum	58
„ membranaceum	58
„ verbascifolium	58
Spatholobus Roxburghii	27
Spiræa callosa	35
Sponia orientalis	72
„ politoria	72
Spondias mangifera	25
Stephania elegans	4
„ rotunda	4
Stephegyne	46
STERCULIACEÆ	10
Sterculia alata	11
„ coccinea	11
„ colorata	11
„ fulgens	11
„ pallens	11
„ villosa	10
Stereospermum chelonoides	58
„ suaveolens	59
Streblus asper	73
Strobilanthes auriculatus	60

	PAGE.
Strobilanthes divaricatus	59
„ maculatus	59
„ pectinatus	59
„ pentstemonoides	60
„ Wallichii	60
STYRACACEÆ	53
Styrax serrulatum	54
Swietenia Mahogani	17
Symplocos caudata	54
„ glomerata	54
„ lucida	54
„ polystachya	54
„ ramosissima	54
„ racemosa	53
„ spicata	54
Syringa vulgaris	55

T.

Tabernæmontana coronaria	55
Talauma Hodgsoni	3
Tamarindus Indica	32
TAMARISCINEÆ	6
Tamarix dioica	6
Tapiria hirsuta	24
Taxus baccata	83
Tectona grandis	60
Tephrosia candida	26
Terminalia belerica	39
„ Chebula	39
„ myriopteron	39
„ tomentosa	39
TERNSTRÖMIACEÆ	7
Tetrameles nudiflora	43
Tetranthera amara	65
„ glauca	65
„ læta	65
„ laurifolia	65
„ monopetala	65
„ polyantha	65
„ salicifolia	65
„ sericea	65
„ tomentosa	65
Teucrium macrostachyum	62
Thamnocalamus Falconeri	87
„ spathiflorus	87
Thespesia lampas	10
Thevetia neriifolia	56
Thuja orientalis	83
Thunbergia coccinea	59
„ fragrans	59
„ grandiflora	59
„ lutea	59
THYMELÆACEÆ	67
TILIACEÆ	12
Tinospora cordifolia	4
Toddalia aculeata	14
Torricellia tiliæfolia	45
Tournefortia viridiflora	57
Trevesia palmata	44
Trewia nudiflora	70
Turpinia Nepalensis	23
„ pomifera	23

U.

Ulex Europæus	34
Ulmus lancifolia	72
Uncaria pilosa	47
„ sessilifructus	47
URTICACEÆ	72
Urtica heterophylla	77
Uvaria macropoda	3

V.

PAGE.

VACCINIACEÆ . . . 50
Vaccinium Dunalianum . . . 50
,, obovatum . . . 50
,, rugosum . . . 50
,, serratum . . . 50
Vangueria spinosa . . . 49
VERBENACEÆ . . . 60
Vernonia volkameriæfolia . . 50
Viburnum coriaceum . . . 46
,, corylifolium . . . 46
,, erubescens . . . 46
,, involucratum . . . 46
,, lutescens . . . 46
,, punctatum . . . 46
Villebrunea appendiculata . . 77
,, frutescens . . . 77
VIOLACEÆ . . . 6
Viscum album . . . 66
,, attenuatum . . . 66
Vitis adnata . . . 20
,, barbata . . . 20
,, bracteolata . . . 20
,, capriolata . . . 20
,, carnosa . . . 20
,, discolor . . . 19
,, elongata . . . 20
,, glauca . . . 20
,, Himalayana . . . 20
,, lanata . . . 20
,, lanceolaria . . . 20

PAGE.

Vitis pedata . . . 21
,, repanda . . . 20
,, rumicisperma . . . 20
,, ternifolia . . . 20
,, vinifera . . . 20
Vitex altissima . . . 61
,, heterophylla . . . 61
,, trifolia . . . 61

W.

Wallichia densiflora . . . 84
,, disticha . . . 84
Wendlandia cinerea . . . 47
,, coriacea . . . 47
,, exserta . . . 48
Wightia gigantea . . . 58
Woodfordia floribunda . . . 42
Wrightia tomentosa . . . 55

Z.

Zanthoxylum acanthopodium . . 14
,, alatum . . . 14
,, Hamiltonianum . . 14
,, ovalifolium . . . 13
,, oxyphyllum . . . 14
Zizyphus Jujuba . . . 19
,, rugosa . . . 19

INDEX OF VERNACULAR NAMES.

A. PAGE.

Achal 19, 68
Achatta 22
Aigiri 60
Ajeru 66
Ajiru 67
Akh 70
Akhaterwa 16, 65
Akhrot 80
Akshi 2
Am 24, 34
Ambhi 24
Amili-lara 52
Amil-pati 53
Amil-taki 31
Ampati-lara 57
Amrut 40
Amuk 40
Amuki 48
Amultas 30
Anar 42
Antabi 49
Aonla 68
Aradi 32
Archal 41
Arkoulo 78
Aru 34
Aryili 67
Asari . . . 48, 55, 57
Asura 69
Asuru 65
Atok-dúng 2
Auk 56

B.

Badulpati 58
Bael 15
Baer 19
Bagverendi 71
Bahera 39
Baichua 62
Bainchampa 49
Bairi-lara 57
Baisi-kara 47
Bajadanti ii
Bakre-lara 48
Balay timur 14
Balengra 27, 28
Ballera 44
Baloo chinia 44
Balphet-kúng 29
Barbari 56
Bander siris 29
Bandka 6
Bandri 6
Bandriphal 16
Bangikat 68, 81

PAGE.

Banj 12
Banj katús 79
Bara champ 3
„ churcheri 20
„ dabdabbi 24
„ jamun 40
„ jhingni 7
„ katús 78
Barbari 56
Basak 38
Batrachi 13
Batúlpati 4
Batwasi 19, 28
Bauriphal 16
Begoha 87
Beis 81
Bejunpati 56
Belari-lara i
Bepari 13, 72
Berikuru 45
Ber-kúng 37
Bet 85
Betlara 45
Bhadras 13
Bhagmili 24
Bhalai 25
Bhayla 25
Bhi 58
Bilauni 52
Bimir 15
Bipemkanta 35
Bleeng 87
Bobich 16
Bodle-kuru 26
Bodle-lara 26
Boeri 57
Bogay timur 14
Bogoti 38, 52
Bohari 57
Boktok-kúng 41
Bolay 23
Bolatrú 27
Bolú 26, 27, 28
Booloo 51
Bop-kúng 58
Bor 73, 74
Borderi 49
Borhar 73
Bor-kúng 86
Borla 31
Borodengri 42
Brong-kúng 25
Brool 85
Brúdúng 26
Brú-rik 26
Budgrat 78
Búk 78

NOTE.—The Lepcha prefix *Hlo* means Hill, and the affixes *kúng, dúng* or *nyok*, and *rik*, mean respectively *tree, soft-wooded shrub* or *climber*, and *climber*. The Paharia prefixes *Oulia, Sanu*, and *Tolu*, are equivalent to *plains, small* and *big*.

PAGE.

Bukainú 16
Bukayun 16
Bulyettra 21
Burgonli 42
Bway champ 69

C.

Cha 9
Chalegachh 16
Chalta 1
Cham 50
Chamo-kúng 54
Chandan 54
Chandang 83
Charu 50
Cha-shing 9, 54
Chatiwan 55
Chatri 5
Chatwan 55
Cheongboo 83
Chepe kúrú 26
Cherinangri 22
Chhota arkoulo 78
" aryili 67
" galeni 49
" kagshi 71
" kimbu 77
" kooail 77
Chiaduk 19
Chikyeng-kúng 19
Chilauni 8, 18
Chilikat 72
Chillay 57
Chimal 51, 52
Ching-kúng 71
Chinia 44, 45
Chinli 5
Chipti kurú 26
Chiringi jhar 25
Chiriya-baug 46
Chiriyanangri 4
Chitú 62
Chongfibrik 56
Chongtafibrik 59
Choori 53
Chonlisy 41
Chua 61
Chuchi am 24
Chukboo 83
Chumlani 14, 53
Chung-kúng 62
Chungkyek-dúm 42
Chungkyek-kúng 60
Churcheri 20
Churipat 48
Chutra 5
Chuwa 41

D.

Dabdabbi 16
Dagdakti 71
Dahiri 42
Dala hurdi 49
Dalné katúa 79
Damar 29
Dampantóm-kúng 21
Danbagla 12
Dangeenrik 57
Dangnosooketek 76
Dangnyinerik 27
Dangsipha-kúng 8
Dangri bet 85
Dansagla 12
Dantaglar 10
Daom-kúng 23
Dar 76
Dayshing 67
Debre-lara 27
Dehua 73
Den-nok 49
Denyok 58
Deomuk 49
Dhup 81
Dombyem 4
Door-kúng 42
Dosúl 63
Dowari 47, 57
Duari-lara 46, 55
Dudela-lara 45
Dudila 75
Dudila-lara 75
Dudhali 55
Dudri 64
Dumri 76
Dumriphal 76
Dumshing 82
Dursal 58

E.

Etok 51
Etokamat 51

F.

Fagiri 68
Femsikól 40
Fatsiphok 85
Filing 87
Flotoshing-rik 3
Flotungchong-kúng 7
Fullidha 27

G.

Galeni 21, 46
Gamari 70
Gambari 61
Gande 67
Ganné 46
Garodosal 29
Garum 70
Gebokanak 38
Geio 69, 70
Gempé aselu 36
Geophul 13
Gia 15
Gineri 60, 61
Giruli 75
Gobia 87
Gobria 12
Goehlo 60
Gogay champ 2
Gogen 8
Goguldhup 15
Gok 3
Gorakuri 46
Gouri bet 85
Guglat 49
Gular 76
Gulsuné 77
Gundrow 48

PAGE.

Gunserai 64
Guras 51, 52
Gurjo 4
Gurupis 62
Gwyheli 61
Gyasay-kúng 75
Gyesa-kúng 27

H.

Hais 5
Harari 33
Harra 39
Harré 3
Hattipaila 11
Hikpi-kúng 25
Himalchiri 53, 69
Himan-kúng 24
Hingman-kúng 23
Hingua 9
Hloprongzam-kúng 44
Hlosablot-kúng 35
Hlosipha-kúng 8
Hloserie-kúng 78
Hlosonli-kúng 79
Hlotagbret 20
Hlotumbrik 36
Huldi-kúng 49
Hurchu 66
Hurdi 49

I.

Iktibi 68
Ikti-kúng 68
Imli 32
Irbo-lara 54

J.

Jagri 68
Jagrikat 64, 71
Jait 26
Jamti 60
Jaman 41
Jamu . . . 40, 41, 54, 75
Jamun 40
Jarila 67
Jarila-lara 20
Jhenok-kúng 1
Jhingni 7
Jhunok-kúng 15
Jogi mallata 70, 71
Jungsong-kúng 40

K.

Kabashi 22, 23
Kachi-kúng 15
Kachik-kúng 31
Kachnar 31
Kadam 46, 71
Kadiwan-rik 58
Kadoo 6
Kadungbi 62
Kadung-nyok 62
Kagbhalai 69
Kaghuti 67
Kagi 25
Kagphulai 24
Kahukrik 47
Kaiday 53

PAGE.

Kainjal 69
Kair-kúng 68
Kajpati 44
Kajutalam 86
Kajúkoprik 28
Kajyang-kúng 43
Kaktay 12
Kala boeri 11
„ bogoti 61
„ champ 2
„ kiamoni 54
„ kharani 64
„ khwairahlo 31
„ siris 84
Kalay 18
Kalay bogoti 53
Kalé 46
Kalé aselu 86
Kaledzo 64
Kalet-kúng 57
Kalhenyok 48
Kalhet-kúng 49
Kali guras 51
Kali-hurchu 50
Kalikat 46
Kali-lara . . . 28, 40, 47, 56
Kalipat 6
Kaljemi 15
Kamaranga 13
Kamhyem-kúng 77
Kamila 70
Kamki 35
Kamla 15
Kamli 76
„ mallata 70, 71
Kanai 76
Kancha-kúng 46
Kangi 48
Kangji-kúng 73
Kanhlyem-kúng 10, 11
Kanhya 76
Kankar 32
Kanom-kúng 39
Kantjer 69
Kautier nyok 22
Kantómnok 21
Kanukpa 13
Kanú-kúng 13
Kanyoo-kúng 64
Kaphal-kúng 11
Kaphalmúk 10
Kaphitki 77
Karam 46
Karima 6
Karingi 55
Karmai 81
Karpati-lara 4
Kashiendúng 78
Kashiorón 79
Kashioshem 79
Kashyem 85
Kasirut 75
Kasonli-lara 5
Kasrekan 75
Kasré maling 87
Kasreto 75
Kasur-kúng 8
Katior-kúng 11
Katong 84
Katongzu 16
Katúr-kúng 24
Katús 78, 79

	Page.
Kawala	64
Kawol	64
Kazu	77
Kegoo	61
Kemoo	51
Kengeni	25
Khair	83
Kharani	54
Kharsoni	63
Kharwa	76
Khola ruis	71
Khour	82
Khur	84
Khwairalo	31
Kiamoni	40
Kimbu	77
Kino	27, ii
Kirima	65
Kirma	77
Kironli	6
Kirra	55
Kisri	7
Kojú-lara	26
Kongki-kúng	25, 34
Kooail	72
Koombooten	50
Koomsoong-kúng	72
Kosrú	23
Kotul kasub	25
Kouatch	27, 28
Kowal-kúng	80
Krim-kúng	65
Kubindé	10
Kucheeng-kúng	78
Kuchiang-kúng	79
Kudmero	65
Kulain	38
Kulyatzo-kúng	53
Kumbi	41
Kumbool-kúng	37
Kumbrong-kúng	14
Kumbyúng	69
Kundoung-kúng	75
Kungchen-rik	20
Kungshior	50
Kúngsúng-kúng	8
Kunhil-kúng	42
Kunhip	74
Kúnsúng-kúng	12
Kuntunrik	57
Kursimla	47
Kusrit	77
Kuttal	73
Kyingbi	77
Kyinki	77
L.	
Labshi	16, 17
Laho-kúng	27
Lajima	32
Lakori	58
Lal champ	2
„ chandan	54
„ galeni	21
„ guras	51
„ kabashi	22
„ kainjal	72
„ mallata	71
„ totilla	44
Lali	64, 73
Lalú	13
Lampatia	42
Lapi	72
Lasmani	14
Lasuni	18
Lat	85
Latikat	68
Lati mahwa	16
Lekbilani	75
Lepchaphal	64
Lesoo	74
Likh-aru	85
Likh Paieli	65
Li-kúng	36, 37
Lilima	77
Lipio	77
Loima-lara	69
Lowri-am	24
Lubbor-kúng	44
Lumbo-kúng	15
Lungom-rik	28
Lut-ter	73
M.	
Madanay	15
Madar	56
Madling-kúng	30
Mahlbans	87
Mahlu	87
Mahow	10
Mahua	81
Maidal	48
Mainakat	43
Maldit-kúng	15
Maling	87
Mallata	71
Malligiri	64
Mandani	43
Mandania	30
Mandani-singhata	3
Mangúpantú-kúng	21
Maniphtyol	26
Manjit	49
Mantet-kúng	41, 70
Mashul-lara	24
Maslara	56
Maspati-lara	27
Matet-kúng	62
Maukap-rik	26
Mehndi	42
Mein kara	14
Mekrap-kúng	77
Michapgong	61
Michapnok	61
Michepnor-kúng	6
Mikrúm-rik	20
Mimri	47
Mipit-múk	28
Momrik	58
Mongthel-kúng	71
Monkakrik	61
Monkyourik	2, 59
Moqchini	44
Moringi	77
Mowa	81
Munkungjor	67
Muntirh	60
Murgut-kúng	23
Murkut-kúng	61
Muslindi	65
Muslini	11
Musré-katús	79
Mya	72
Myungarer-rik	4

	Page.
N.	
Nagpat	23
Naitijemi	15
Naiwilli-lara	81
Nalgi	12
Nali	6
Nambroongkor	70
Namjil	71
Namosinglet-kúng	27
Namro-kúng	71
Nandiki	13
Naringi	15
Narokpa	15
Naski	5
Natkanta	15
Neet-kúng	81
Neri	61
Newarpati	56
Ngræm-kúng	33
Ngrœm-rik	33
Nilay	12
Nimat-kúng	57
Nimbor	15
Nimi-lara	4
Numbong-kúng	46, 70
Numboongkor	70
Number-kúng	61
Numbyong-kúng	77
Numingrik	36
Number-kúng	41
Nunewalai	24
Nupsor-kúng	63, 65
O.	
Ooh	84
Orer	71
Oulia champ	3
„ kharani	54
Ouli gogen	8
Owla	68
P.	
Paddam	34
Padebiri	49
Pagjiokpo	87
Pahar-lampati	53
Paieli	65
Paili	68
Pajpati	61
Pakar	75
Pakjik	88
Pakpa	88
Palamkat	39
Palap-kúng	70
Palasi	27
Palass	27
Palegnyok	22
Palé-kúng	22
Palet-kúng	45
Paletnyok	45
Palok-kúng	72
Palyok-kúng	53, 54
Pandoor-kúng	46
Panji-kung	48
Pangla	4
Pangra	32
Pani-lara	20
Pantóm	21
Pao	87
Paowlay	14
Papita	43
Paphok	87
Papoi	43
Papray-lara	58
Parari	58, 59
Pari	48
Parirajhar	55
Pashien	88
Patimil	69
Patlé katus	78, 79
Patmero	64
Patmoro	45
Patpatta	3
Payir-rik	33
Payo-kúng	76
Payomko-kúng	43
Payong	87
Payongrik	23, 53
Payúng	79
Pendder	2
Pengji-kúng	69
Phalat	78
Phamlet	65
Phamlet-kung	64, 65
Phamsikol	1
Phase-kúng	65
Phani-kúng	64
Phekri galeni	21
Phirphiri	11
Phober-kúng	40
Phota	44
Phugong-kúng	19
Phul amphi	45
Phusri	65
Phusri kamli	70
„ mallata	76
Phyeum	87
Piazay	50
Pindik	40
Pinri	47
Pipal	75
Pipli	38, 75
Pitamari	48
Poguntig	70
Pohong	36
Pohor-kúng	65
Pondam-kúng	56
Pooalay	65
Pooteli	65
Pronchadik	4
Prong	87
Prongnok	86
Prongzam-kúng	6, 44, 45
Prongzamnyok	44
Proosti	66
Pua	76
Pudlikat	72
Pugriang	88
Pukshioungrik	85
Pundri-kúng	5
Purbo-kúng	55
Purbong	86
Purbongnyok	5
Pureni	20
Purgeen-rik	56
Purmo-kúng	52
Puroa-kúng	70
Purpuray timur	14
Púrúni	77
Puya	77
Pyashing	56

	Page.
R.	
Rabi bet	85
Rabu-lara	8
Raj birij	80
Rajlok-kúng	71
Raniwalai	24
Rata gogen	8
Ratay	50
Ratmanti	65
Reem	85
Rha-kúng	31
Robbay	38
Rodinga	27
Rohu-kúng	64
Ronchiling-kúng	25
Romchiling-rik	24
Rong	85
Rotdhip	62
Rue	85
Rusbee	85
Ruglim-rik	18
Rukh baer	19
Rungbong	84
Runggong	80
Rungyeongrik	19
Runool	85
Ryôm	56
S.	
Sadun	80
Safed champ	8
„ kabra	75
Safednyok	65
Safed siris	83
Saj	39
Sakwa	9
Sâl	9
Sali-lara	11
Samli	23
Sanakadan-kúng	6
Sané	8
Sané aselu	36
Sanging-kúng	63
Sangji-kúng	76
Sani dudela	76
Sanu hingo	54
„ jhingni	7
„ kabashi	11
„ kimu	18
„ pureni	19
Saphiji-rik	14
Saré gogen	8
Sarputtia	62
Sauer	80
Saver	79
Schiap	86
Sealposra	12
Sedangtaglar	10
Sedeng	76
Sedong-kúng	33, 34
Sedong-tagla	72
Sehshing	82
Selemnyok	55
Sema-kúng	38
Sempat	65
Semul	10
Senén-kúng	77
Sentungrúng	69
Serh-kúng	24
Serhnyok	24
Shariphal	8

	Page.
Shechin	59, 62
Shedbarwa	67
Shempati	13
Shengrik	29
Shimbeng-nyok	35
Shitzem-kúng	14
Shubung-lara	13
Shukni-kúng	2
Shumbul-kúng	37
Siamunú	23
Sibri	70
Sibriú-kúng	32
Sida	42
Sidemnyok	15
Siffoo-kúng	3
Sigugrip	3
Sigumgrip	2
Silhokmongú	16
Silim-kúng	39
Silot-kúng	16
Siltimber	65
Silum-kúng	15
Simali	14
Simali-lara	23
Simal-kúng	16
Simbrangrip	47
Simong	84
Simplet búk	56
Simplút-rik	13
Sinakadang-kúng	16
Sindri-lara	61
Sindooria	70
Singhani	87
Singbatta	43
Singhatta-lara	3, 44
Singka	37
Sing-kúng	71
Singliang-kúng	38
Singna	45
Singnamook	38
Singnok	48
Singnok-kúng	3, 23
Singoli	63
Singriang-kúng	34
Singtok	77
Singyen	53
Singyen-kúng	58, 59
Sinong-kúng	69
Sivor-kúng	58
Sionsoon-kúng	73
Siora	73
Sipha-kúng	8
Siphokji	35
Siratpé	75
Sirhootúngcher	22
Sirikishu	79
Siri-kúng	78, 79
Siriokhytem-kúng	43, 44
Siris	33
Sirisi jhar	26
Sirispanterr-kúng	21
Siritakdangji	14, 36
Sisi	65
Sissú	28
Sitisal	29
Sitsal	29
Sitnyok	75
Sivettachim	62
Sivor-kúng	58
Somri	43
Sua	60
Sufhyi-kúng	66

PAGE.

Suglim-kúng 18
Sugribong-kúng 81
Sugroo-mook 60
Sugvat-kúng 42
Súhútúngrúng 26
Suhutúngrúng-rik 31
Sukurruglim-rik 19
Sambling-kúng 69
Sumbrong kúng 8
Sumcher-kúng 60
Sunakhari 56
Sundok-kúng 48
Sung-a-kúng 60
Sungden-kúng 4
Sungli-kúng 80
Sungloch-kúng 39
Sunglokvar rik 40
Sungloo-kúng 10
Sunglyer-nyok 6
Sungna-kúng 61
Sungnem-kúng 41
Sungrú-kúng 14
Sungoo-rik 18
Sungray 30
Sungtong-kúng 44
Sungungrik 31
Sunkong-kúng 73
Sunkrong 77
Sunom-kúng 41
Sunn 25
Suntala 15
Suntri 5
Suntúngrúngrik 18
Suom-kúng 68
Supari 84
Suphút-kúng 65
Suppatnyok 65
Surool 64
Suviak-kúng 81

T.

Takbli-rik 20
Takbret-kúng 76, 77
Takchabrik 70
Takchirnyok 48
Takhril-kúng 24
Taki 31
Takmur-kúng 33
Taknyeé-rik 28
Takoru 84
Takpa 79
Takpadik 57
Takpo-kúng 34
Takpœdrik 49
Takpyit-kúng 34
Takpyit-múk 25
Takpyit-nyok 34
Takri bet 86
Taksielrik 3
Taksor-kúng 12, 39
Taksot-rik 75
Taksur 76
Taktokhyem 32
Talainyom 86
Tangarook-kúng 16
Tangshing 83
Tanki-kúng 43
Tapathyer 45
Tapyit-nyok 31
Tarsing 84
Tatebiri 29

Tstri 2
Tchongtay-kúng 76
Tedong-kúng 33
Tenga-lara 67
Teihyaprik 29
Terhil-nyok 15
Terhilsok-kúng 65
Terolrik 27
Tetrikair-kúng 68
Teturldumm 38
Teturl-kúng 9
Thali 23
Thali kabashi 22
Tikiphal 8
Tikphal 8
Tilgia 47
Tilhetter 44
Tilki 47
Timbur 14
Timburjhien 5
Timburnyok 14, 54
Timil 45, 76
Timur 14
Tirhyuk-myok 26
Titapat 50
Titi nigala 86
Titri 32
Toldúng 33
Tol-rik 33
Tolu aselu 35
Tong-or-kúng 62
Tou-nyok 29
Topatnyok 59
Totilla 59
Totnye 63
Tsa 83
Tsema 5
Tsemangri 21
Tshithé 75
Tsitpay 75
Tugla kúng 73
Tugom-kúng 62
Tukbretrik 20
Tukbrinyok 20
Túk-kúng 6
Tuksat-kúng 72
Tuksot-kúng 75, 76
Tuksingrik 8
Tumberh-kúng 48
Tumbomri 6
Tumbrúng-kúng 18
Tumbrúngrik 19
Tumbuk 45
Tungbongrik 1
Tungbram-kúng 41
Tungcheong-kúng 52, 54
Tungcheongmonrik 19
Tungcher-kúng 69
Tungchir-kúng 15
Tungchir-rik 13
Tungchong-kúng 7
Tungflam-kúng 70
Tunggor-rik 5
Tungnyok-kúng 22
Tungrangmúk 58
Tungrong-rik 57
Tungru-kúng 37
Tungrung-kúng 54
Tungrootrik 20
Tungrootrikup 21
Tungshing 43
Tunguk-kúng 46

	Page.
Tuni	16, 17
Tushiari	77
U.	
Udal	10
Ullo	77
Unyo	88
Utis	80
V.	
Vhyem	49
Vhym-rik	20
Y.	
Yalishin	22
Yangkup	30
Yatli-kúng	23
Yel-kúng	63
Yeinyo	87
Yi-kúng	61
Yok	74
Yokchoung-rik	55, 56
Yokdung	74